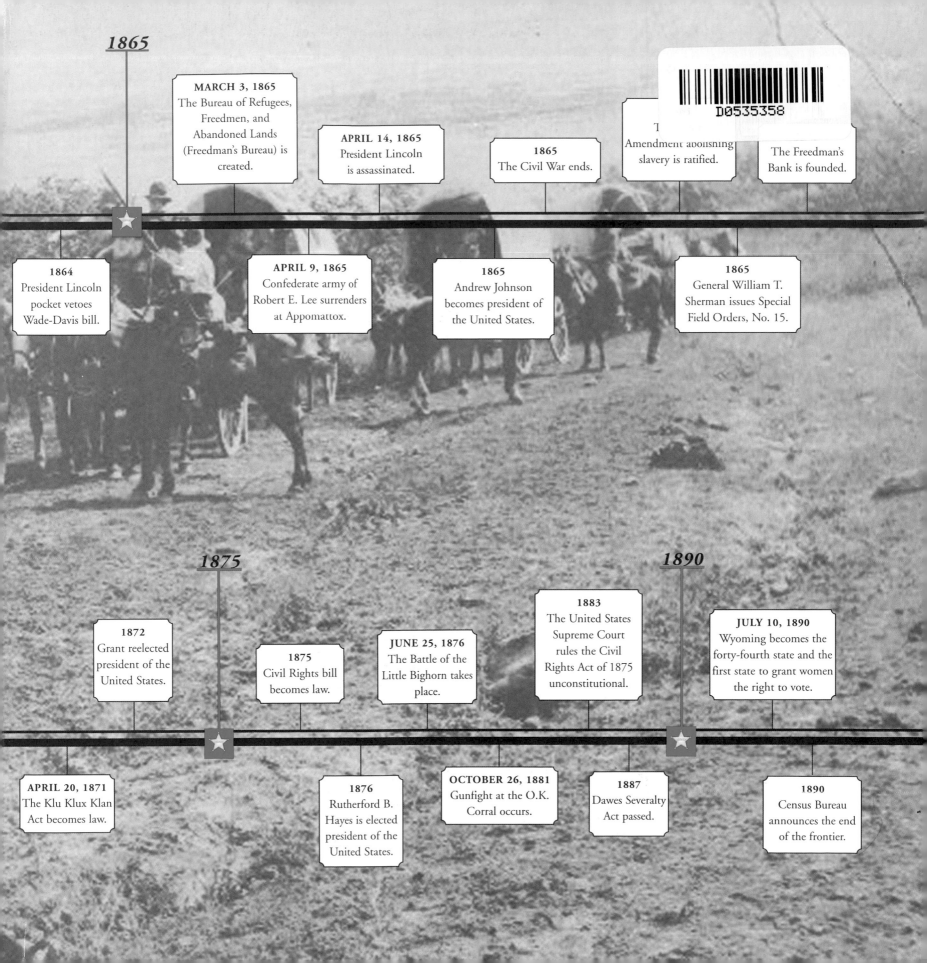

1865

MARCH 3, 1865
The Bureau of Refugees, Freedmen, and Abandoned Lands (Freedman's Bureau) is created.

APRIL 14, 1865
President Lincoln is assassinated.

1865
The Civil War ends.

Amendment abolishing slavery is ratified.

The Freedman's Bank is founded.

1864
President Lincoln pocket vetoes Wade-Davis bill.

APRIL 9, 1865
Confederate army of Robert E. Lee surrenders at Appomattox.

1865
Andrew Johnson becomes president of the United States.

1865
General William T. Sherman issues Special Field Orders, No. 15.

1875

1890

1872
Grant reelected president of the United States.

1875
Civil Rights bill becomes law.

JUNE 25, 1876
The Battle of the Little Bighorn takes place.

1883
The United States Supreme Court rules the Civil Rights Act of 1875 unconstitutional.

JULY 10, 1890
Wyoming becomes the forty-fourth state and the first state to grant women the right to vote.

APRIL 20, 1871
The Klu Klux Klan Act becomes law.

1876
Rutherford B. Hayes is elected president of the United States.

OCTOBER 26, 1881
Gunfight at the O.K. Corral occurs.

1887
Dawes Severalty Act passed.

1890
Census Bureau announces the end of the frontier.

D0535358

INTO THE WEST

FROM RECONSTRUCTION TO THE FINAL DAYS OF THE AMERICAN FRONTIER

James M. McPherson

A BYRON PREISS VISUAL PUBLICATIONS, INC., BOOK

ATHENEUM BOOKS FOR YOUNG READERS

NEW YORK · LONDON · TORONTO · SYDNEY

To Anne Schaeffer Long

Atheneum Books for Young Readers
An imprint of Simon & Schuster Children's
Publishing Division
1230 Avenue of the Americas
New York, New York 10020

Copyright © 2006 by James M. McPherson

Front jacket photo caption: The Oregon Trail by N. C.
Wyeth, copyright © 1925.

All rights reserved, including the right of reproduction
in whole or in part in any form.

Book design by Edie Weinberg
The text of this book was set in AGaramond.

Manufactured in the United States of America
First Edition

10 9 8 7 6 5 4 3 2 1

Library of Congress Cataloging-in-Publication Data
McPherson, James M.
Into the west: from Reconstruction to the final days of the
American frontier / James M. McPherson.—1st ed.
p.   cm.
ISBN-13: 978-0-689-86543-5
ISBN-10: 0-689-86543-0
1. West (U.S.)—History—1860–1890—Juvenile literature.
2. Reconstruction (U.S. history, 1865–1877)–Juvenile lit-
erature. 3. United States—History—1865–1898—Juvenile
literature. 4. Froniter and pioneer life—West (U.S.)—Juvenile
literature. 5. Cowboys—West (U.S.)—19th century—
History—Juvenile literature. 6. Indians of North America—
Wars—West (U.S.)—Juvenile literature. 7. Indians of North
America—Wars—1886–1895—Juvenile literature. I. Title.
F594.M25 2006
978'.02—dc22   2005026024

PHOTO CREDITS
Denver Public Library, Western History Collection, X-21803:
p. 14
Denver Public Library, Western History Collection, X-21939:
p. 56
Denver Public Library, Western History Collection, MCC-
1848: p. 57
Denver Public Library, Western History Collection, X-21930:
p. 58
Denver Public Library, Western History Collection, X-31308:
p. 74
Denver Public Library, Western History Collection, X-31466:
p. 84
Denver Public Library, Western History Collection, Z-112:
p. 85
Fred Hultstrand History in Pictures Collection, NDIRS-
NDSU, Fargo: p. 45
Library of Congress: pp. 6, 8, 9, 11, 12, 15, 18, 19, 20, 21, 22,
23, 24, 28, 30, 31, 32, 36, 37, 40, 41, 42, 43, 50, 52, 53,
54, 55, 60, 61, 65, 68, 69, 70, 71, 73, 75, 76, 78, 79, 80,
81, 83, and 87
National Archives: pp. 7, 16, 17, 35, 48, 72, 82, and 86
Nebraska State Historical Society Photograph Collections:
p. 13
New York Public Library: p. 38
South Dakota State Historical Society-State Archives: p. 34
The Granger Collection, New York: pp. 10, 25, 26, 27, 33, 39,
44, 46, 47, 49, 51, 62, 63, 64, 66, 67, 77, 88, and 89
Union Pacific Historical Collection: p. 29

CONTENTS

From the beginning of the Civil War, the North had fought to "reconstruct" the Union. President Abraham Lincoln first tried to restore the Union as it had existed before 1861, but once the abolition of slavery became a war aim of the North, the nation could never be reconstructed on its old foundations. Instead it needed to experience a "new birth of freedom," as Lincoln had said in 1863 at the dedication of the military cemetery at Gettysburg.

Exactly what did a "new birth of freedom" mean? At the very least it meant the end of slavery. The slave states would be reconstructed on a free-labor basis. In December 1865, the Thirteenth Amendment to the Constitution was ratified, ending slavery in the United States, but what would liberty mean for the four million freed slaves? Would they become citizens equal to their former masters in the eyes of the law? Would Confederate leaders be punished for treason? On what terms would the Confederate states return to the Union? What would be the powers of the states and of the national government in a reconstructed Union? The answers to these and other questions were not easy, nor always successful, as this book will show.

From 1865 to 1870, Congress and President Andrew Johnson (who had become president when Lincoln was assassinated) tried to answer these questions. These years were marked by bitter conflict between the Republican congressional majority and President Johnson, a former Democrat from Tennessee whom the Republicans had nominated for vice president in 1864 to reach out beyond their usual constituency. Johnson vetoed many bills that Congress passed for these purposes and did his best to defeat the Fourteenth Amendment to the Constitution, which granted equal rights to all, regardless of race. Congress enacted the laws over his vetoes and also sent the Fourteenth Amendment to the states, where it was ratified by 1868. Johnson then tried to thwart the enforcement of these laws in Southern states. The House of Representatives finally impeached Johnson in 1868, but he was saved from conviction and removal by the margin of a single vote in the Senate.

Northern war hero Ulysses S. Grant was elected president in 1868. Grant enforced Reconstruction measures in the South against the violent resistance of terrorist organizations such as the Ku Klux Klan and the White League. By 1875, however, many Northerners had grown tired of or alarmed by the continued intervention of federal troops in Southern affairs.

In 1877 newly elected President Rutherford B. Hayes withdrew the soldiers from the South, bringing an end to a ten-year period known as Reconstruction. During these years the government had achieved two of the three goals of Reconstruction: 1. to reincorporate the former Confederate states into the Union and 2. to accomplish a transition from slavery to freedom in the South. However, that transition was marred by the emergence of racial inequality, sharecropping, and white supremacy in the post-Reconstruction South. The third goal of Reconstruction, enforcement of equal civil and political rights promised in the Fourteenth and Fifteenth Amendments, would have to await the "second Reconstruction" of the civil rights movement almost a century later.

Despite the nation's preoccupation with Reconstruction, one of the most remarkable developments of this era was the rapid expansion of the western frontier. From 1865 to 1890, the white population west of the ninety-fifth meridian (roughly a line from Galveston, Texas, through Kansas City, Missouri, to Bemidji, Minnesota) increased by 400 percent to 8,628,000, a growth rate five times greater than the nation's growth as a whole. As much new agricultural and grazing land came under cultivation and use by white Americans during those 25 years as during the previous 250 years.

One of the main engines of this postwar expansion was the railroad. Five transcontinental railroads went into service between 1869 and 1893. At the end of the Civil War, only 3,272 miles of rail ran west of the Mississippi River. By 1890 the total was 72,473 miles. Railroad access and mobility spurred settlement and economic development on the high plains and in the mountain valleys.

This was the age of the sodbusters, pioneers who adapted to the almost treeless prairies and plains by fencing

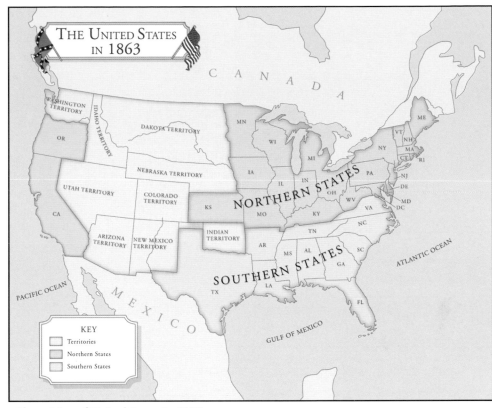

Above: Map of United States in 1880.

land with barbed wire and building houses with sod broken with the plow. Even more important to the growth of the West, and surely more celebrated in song and story, were the mining and ranching frontiers. This was the West of prospectors and boomtowns, of cowboys and cattle drives, of gold rushes and mother lodes, of stagecoach robbers and rustlers. It was a West so romanticized that it is hard to separate myth from reality. As a boy I watched dozens of Western movies starring Gene Autry, Roy Rogers, and Hopalong Cassidy, which were filled with myths. When I grew up and became a historian, it was surprising to learn the realities of the West, which I have tried to present to you in this book.

Though exciting and necessary, this westward expansion came at great cost to some groups. The American Indians, now known as Native Americans, were despoiled of their remaining open land and herded onto reservations. Buffalo were hunted almost to extinction.

In 1890 the superintendent of the U.S. Census made a sober announcement of dramatic import: "Up to and including 1880 the country had a frontier of settlement, but at present the unsettled area has been so broken into by isolated bodies of settlement that there can hardly be said to be a frontier line . . . any longer." An era of American history that began with the arrival of the first Europeans in the sixteenth century had come to an end. While the American frontier no longer existed, its spirit and the larger-than-life men and women who explored and settled it continue to capture the imagination.

James M. McPherson

Above: Five generations of African Americans who lived as slaves on a plantation in Beaufort, South Carolina.

QUICK FACTS

★ The Republican Party was less than 10 years old when the Civil War began. It had been founded in 1854. Though Lincoln was the first Republican president, he was the second Republican to run for the office. In 1856 explorer John C. Frémont had been the first Republican presidential candidate. He lost to Democrat James Buchanan.

★ When the Civil War ended, 13-year-old Caroline Cowles Richards woke in New York to the sound of bells tolling: "Lee has surrendered! [A]nd all the people seem crazy in consequence. The bells are ringing, boys and girls, men and women are running through the streets wild with excitement; the flags are all flying, one from the top of our church, and such a 'hurrah boys' generally, I never dreamed of."

The American Civil War (1861–1865) almost destroyed the United States. The main cause of the war was slavery, which was originally deemed acceptable in the main text of the U.S. Constitution. In the years following the country's birth in 1776, Northern states gradually abolished slavery for economic and moral reasons.

In the South slavery continued to endure. Though slaves worked in a wide variety of businesses, they had especially become an integral part of the agricultural economy that dominated the region. Slavery gave the cotton plantation owners an inexpensive source of labor with which to harvest crops.

As the nation expanded westward and new states were added, the balance of power between the free states in the North and the slave states of the South became more and more strained. Northern states wanted to limit the expansion of slavery in the new territory, and Southern states did not. The two most important pieces of legislation that tried to peacefully reconcile the problem were the Missouri Compromise and the Compromise of 1850, both of which controlled where and how slavery would be allowed. Neither side was happy with the results of the compromises, but they were not yet willing to go to war to settle the issue once and for all.

That feeling changed when Abraham Lincoln was elected president in 1860. Many Southerners hated Lincoln, because they believed he was anti-slavery and wanted to eliminate it in the South. Before he was inaugurated, seven slave states—South Carolina, Mississippi, Florida, Alabama, Georgia, Louisiana, and Texas—voted to break away from the United States and create their own country, the Confederate States of America, with Jefferson Davis as its president.

Soon after Lincoln was sworn in as president, Confederate forces attacked the federal installation at Fort Sumter, South Carolina, on April 12, 1861, starting the Civil War. Less than two months later, the slave states of Virginia, Tennessee, Arkansas, and North Carolina joined the Confederacy. Throughout the conflict, Lincoln steadfastly maintained that the states of the Confederacy had never left the Union. However, it would take four years and the lives of more than 620,000 Union and Confederate soldiers—as well as the life of Lincoln himself—before his belief could once again become a reality. When the war ended in 1865, one question loomed large: How would the victorious North restore and rebuild a shattered country?

Opposite: Union soldiers at camp near Antietam, Maryland.

Above: The End of the Rebellion in the United States, 1865, a nineteenth-century lithograph by C. Kimmel.

QUICK FACT

☆ One of Congress's attempts to impose reconstruction was the Wade-Davis bill of 1864, which punished the states that had seceded more severely than Lincoln's program. Congress passed the legislation near the end of its session. Lincoln didn't like the measure and did not want it to become law. At the same time, he did not want to veto it because that might create other political problems for him. Instead he used what is called the "pocket veto," which requires the president to sign any bill brought before him within ten days after the adjournment of a congressional session. If he does not sign it, the bill does not become law. It is vetoed, but without the formality of a negative signature. Lincoln used a pocket veto on the Wade-Davis bill.

On November 19, 1863, President Lincoln delivered his Gettysburg Address. That speech capped a memorial ceremony held in Pennsylvania where, five months earlier, Union and Confederate forces had fought the greatest battle in the war. In his speech, Lincoln used the word "nation" five times. In previous speeches and correspondence, instead of "nation," he had used the word "Union." Though the word "Union" came to be associated with the North, that was not Lincoln's intent. He changed the wording because of his desire to announce a new birth of freedom and nationalism for the entire United States of America.

Though much hard fighting lay ahead, the Confederate defeats at Gettysburg (July 1–3, 1863) and Vicksburg (July 4, 1863) and later at Chattanooga (November 23–25, 1863) made increasing numbers of people in the South unhappy with the progress of the war. This encouraged Lincoln, who saw their disaffection as an opportunity to encourage them to return. On December 8, 1863, Lincoln announced a proclamation that described his plan for how seceded states could be reorganized and readmitted to the Union, a plan he called "Reconstruction." Before rebuilding the devastated cities and shattered economy of the South, Lincoln knew he first had to reunite the country.

Lincoln offered pardon and amnesty to anyone who took an oath of allegiance to the United States and to all of its laws and proclamations concerning slavery. The only people ineligible for this amnesty were Confederate government officials and high-ranking military leaders. Whenever the number of people in any state taking the oath reached 10 percent of the number of voters registered in 1860—the last year of national elections before the war began—these voters could organize a state government that the president would recognize as legal. The recognition of federal senators and congressmen was a separate matter because only Congress had that right. Instead of taking a hard line designed to punish the South, Lincoln chose to be generous. His 10 percent plan was deliberately designed to encourage as many people as possible to return to the Union.

From the time the war began, a power struggle existed between the president and Congress over which branch would control the process of rebuilding the country. During the two years after Reconstruction was announced, Congress discussed a number of programs. Though Lincoln

Opposite: Freedmen in a town in the South shortly after the end of the war. Note in the background the battle-scarred buildings.

Above: Presidential election day in New York in November 1864.

QUICK FACTS

☆ The Civil War has a number of names. The government's official history, compiled in the 1880s, called it the "War of the Rebellion." It's also known as the "War Between the States" and the "War Against Northern Aggression."

☆ Many historians consider the Civil War to be the first modern war. A number of inventions were used for the first time to help fight the war, including railroads; armor-clad, steam-powered ships; primitive machine guns; and telegraph communications.

☆ The Democratic Party was the party of opposition during this period. Most Southerners were Democrats, and some important Northern Democratic congressmen and senators had tried to arrange a peace treaty with the Confederacy during the war. As a result many voters in the North regarded the party as the "party of traitors."

had seized the initiative with his proclamation, the matter of how to actually make it work was still not settled. Some members of Congress, including Massachusetts senator Charles Sumner, claimed that secession was an act of treason. As such, they felt Southern states had committed "state suicide," or had ceased to exist as states and reverted to the condition of territories. If Lincoln agreed with this idea, then it would mean that Congress, through its constitutional authority to govern territories and admit new states, would be in charge of Reconstruction and its terms and conditions.

Lincoln publicly took the position that only the federal government, not individual citizens, could dissolve state status. This allowed him to retain power over Reconstruction under his constitutional authority to suppress insurrection and to grant pardons and amnesty.

Lincoln's 10 percent plan dismayed radical Republicans. Pennsylvania Congressman Thaddeus Stevens, one of Lincoln's biggest opponents on the issue, stated, "The foundation of [Southern] institutions . . . must be broken up and relaid, or all our blood and treasure have been spent in vain." Lincoln was not to be moved from his position, though he did claim to be flexible, stating that his plan of amnesty and restoration "is the best the Executive can suggest, with his present impressions, it must not be understood that no other [plan] would be acceptable."

While Congress continued to debate, Lincoln acted. Portions of Tennessee, Louisiana, and Arkansas were by this time under Union control. General Nathaniel Banks, commander of Union occupation forces in Louisiana, agreed with Lincoln's desire for leniency. In a letter to Lincoln he wrote, "The history of the world shows that Revolutions which are not controlled, and held within reasonable limits, produce counter Revolutions We are not likely to prove an exception."

On February 22, 1864, an election was held in the Union-held territory under the proclamation's guidelines. The Arkansas election created a new constitution, which abolished slavery and established a new state government. This election generated about one-fourth of the total vote of 1860. The elections in Louisiana and Tennessee had turnouts of more than 10 percent of the voters. So it appeared that Lincoln's 10 percent plan was working. Lincoln recognized the new governments in these states.

Opposite: A Freedman school in Beaufort, South Carolina.

THE HOMESTEAD ACT

Ho for Kansas!

Brethren, Friends, & Fellow Citizens:
I feel thankful to inform you that the
REAL ESTATE
AND
Homestead Association,
Will Leave Here the
15th of April, 1878,
In pursuit of Homes in the Southwestern
Lands of America, at Transportation
Rates, cheaper than ever
was known before.
For full information inquire of
Benj. Singleton, better known as old Pap,
NO. 5 NORTH FRONT STREET.
Beware of Speculators and Adventurers, as it is a dangerous thing
to fall in their hands.
Nashville, Tenn., March 18, 1878.

Above: A broadside advertising land in Kansas.

12

QUICK FACTS

⭐ During those years the Homestead Act remained in affect, with amendments, in the 48 contiguous United States until 1976. A provision extended the act for an additional 10 years for land in Alaska. During the years of its existence, the Homestead Act helped settle between 270-285 million acres, or roughly 8 percent of the land in the United States.

⭐ African-American homesteaders who settled in Kansas and Oklahoma called themselves "Exodusters." A former slave, Benjamin Singleton, recruited approximately 300 African Americans for homesteading in a community he had formed in Cherokee County in southeastern Kansas.

When the Civil War began, the federal government was land-rich but people-poor in the West. Millions of acres of potential farmland were lying fallow, because there were no people there to farm it. Earlier attempts to provide incentives for settlement were thwarted by a political power struggle over the slavery issue between the North and the South. However, the secession of the slave states in the South gave President Lincoln the opportunity he needed to finally open the frontier for settlement. On May 20, 1862, Lincoln signed into law the Homestead Act, which took effect on January 1, 1863. In order to own 160 acres of land, a U.S. citizen (man or woman), or a person intending to become a U.S. citizen, only had to pay filing fees and commissions totaling eighteen dollars, live on the property for five years, and make some improvements on the land. States and railroads would also receive land grants from the federal government. It was a land-distribution program that had enormous impact. Hundreds of thousands of people settled and cultivated land and created towns in the trackless prairie.

Daniel Freeman was one of the first people to file a land claim under the act. Legend has it that Freeman, a Union army scout in the Nebraska Territory, convinced a land office official to open shortly before midnight of December 31, 1862. As the story goes, he filed his claim at 12:10 A.M. on January 1, 1863. Five years later, on January 20, 1868, an assessment was filed on the property. It noted that Freeman had built a house that was "part log and part panel 14 by 20 foot one story with two doors, two windows, shingle roof, board floors and is a comfortable house to live in." Additionally he "ploughed, fenced, and cultivated about 35 acres of . . . land and made the following improvements thereon, to wit: built a stable, a . . . shed, 100 foot long corn crib, and has 40 apple and about 400 peach trees set out." Freeman received his title deed to the property: "Certificate No. 1" for "Application No. 1" that same day.

However, ownership of land did not guarantee an individual's success. As many farmers in the Great Plains discovered, 160 acres was not enough land to make a good living. Still, the opportunity alone for anyone—man or woman, black or white—to own property was a profound lure. By 1890, approximately 370,000 homesteads on roughly forty-eight million acres had been filed.

Opposite: A homestead family in a sod house in Nebraska. Note the wagon carrying extra blocks of sod.

Above: A pre–Civil War group of Colorado gold rush prospectors in 1860, heading toward the gold fields near Pike's Peak.

QUICK FACTS

⭐ Some of the larger cities on the frontier included Denver, Colorado Territory, (1870 population: 4,759); Bismarck, Dakota Territory, (1874 population: 1,200); and Cheyenne, Wyoming Territory, (1867 population: 4,000).

⭐ The discoveries of gold and silver deposits in California and Nevada, before the Civil War, caused many men to cross the frontier to seek their fortune in the West.

⭐ California, Oregon, Nevada, and Kansas were all states by 1865. So, though they were a part of the West, they were technically not a part of the frontier.

14

Driven by economic necessity, the original Thirteen Colonies along the Atlantic Coast looked east to the mother country of England for financial gain. However, they knew that their future survival and growth lay in the opposite direction, in the West. Even before the American Revolution, colonists had crossed the rugged Appalachian and Allegheny mountain ranges, hunted, trapped, and traded with the Native Americans and carved out settlements and farms in the fertile land of the Ohio River valley and its tributaries. In the years that followed the American Revolution, the young United States, through purchase, war, and annexation expanded westward at a breathtaking pace. By 1848, seventy-two years after independence, the country bordered the Pacific Ocean.

This land grab was given the name "Manifest Destiny" in 1845 by journalist John Louis O'Sullivan, who wrote in a newspaper column, "The American claim is by right of our manifest destiny to overspread and to possess the whole of the continent which Providence has given us. It is a right such as that of the tree to the space of air and earth suitable for the full expansion of its principle and destiny of growth."

At the start of the Civil War, the frontier was considered the section of the country extending from the Mississippi River in the east to the Sierra Nevada Mountains in the west, and from Canada in the north to Texas and Mexico in the south. Further settlement of the area was interrupted by the Civil War. When the war ended, the flow of settlers resumed.

Emily Towell was fifty-two years old when she and her husband became homesteaders. She noted, "Every imagination was fired with dreams and visions of new homes and fortunes to be made in the Fertile West." However, the dream did not come without other costs. Climate and weather, hard work, isolation, and boredom were but a few of the challenges the new settlers encountered. Yet so strong was the belief in Manifest Destiny that men, ranging from the president of the United States to the dispossessed ex-Confederate soldier, saw the frontier as a wilderness waiting to be tamed and cultivated by civilized man.

Opposite: A wagon train pulled by oxen.

THE FIRST SETTLERS: THE NATIVE AMERICANS

Above: An Arapaho camp in the 1870s in Kansas. Note the buffalo meat drying on the poles.

QUICK FACTS

⭐ A number of Native Americans fought on both sides in the Civil War. One of them was Cherokee chief, Stand Watie, who became a brigadier general for the Confederacy. On June 23, 1865, he was the last Confederate commander to surrender.

⭐ Though Native Americans had lived here for thousands of years, they did not officially become citizens of the United States until the twentieth century. Before that, their legal status and rights changed, depending on the treaties signed.

⭐ Plains Indians did not use wheels for transportation. Cargo was dragged behind pack animals on simple but effective triangular-shaped carts called "travois."

European explorers, beginning with Columbus in 1492, discovered that the New World was inhabited by indigenous peoples they called "Indians," and who are today also known as "Native Americans." It is widely accepted that ancestors of these Native Americans had made the prehistoric trek on foot across the land bridge that once connected present-day Russia and Alaska. From there they spread in all directions, some eventually reaching the southern tip of South America. Though the Europeans regarded them as savages, the tribes had distinct civilizations and societies.

An estimated one million Native Americans were living in what would become the United States when Columbus reached the West Indies. By 1860, that number had shrunk to an estimated three hundred thousand.

Disease brought by the Europeans was the biggest culprit in the decline of the Native American population. Smallpox, measles, whooping cough, and other diseases common in Europe were unknown in the New World. Because they lacked immunity, even a relatively mild disease, such as the measles, proved deadly to the Native Americans. Agricultural tribes in the Great Plains, who didn't roam like the nomadic Sioux, were particularly vulnerable. Disease epidemics reduced the Arikara population by 80 percent. Other Great Plains tribes, such as the Hidatsas, Mandans, Omahas, and Poncas, were all but wiped out.

The arrival of the horse, which was introduced by the Spanish in the 1500s, transformed Indian cultures. Most affected were the nomadic Plains tribes. They were able to better follow the buffalo herds upon which they depended for everything from food (meat), shelter (hides for tepees), tools (bones), and fuel (dried manure).

White traders also brought goods that they traded to Native Americans for animal hides, including guns, metal knives and utensils, and cloth. Because traders were few and often seasonal, relationships between the tribes and traders were usually peaceful. However, in the years leading up to the Civil War, the Plains Indians began to resent the flow of people traveling through their land to California and Oregon. Sporadic incidents of violence began to occur between the two groups. After the Civil War ended in 1865 and the stream of white people going west became a flood, a number of the Plains Indian tribes realized that they would have to fight to keep their land.

Opposite: An Ute boy and warrior in northwest Utah.

ASSASSINATION OF PRESIDENT ABRAHAM LINCOLN

Above: President Abraham Lincoln.

QUICK FACTS

⭐ Booth had been a member of the Virginia militia in 1859 and witnessed the execution of abolitionist John Brown.

⭐ Booth originally plotted to kidnap Lincoln and hand him over to the Confederates.

⭐ One of the most tragic figures in the Lincoln assassination was alleged conspirator Dr. Samuel Mudd. Mudd was arrested when it was discovered that he had set Booth's broken leg. Tried as a conspirator, even though he had nothing to do with the plot itself, Mudd was sentenced to life in prison. He was pardoned in 1869. The expression, "His name is mud," referring to someone in serious trouble, has its origins in Mudd's misfortune.

On April 9, 1865, after four long years of war, the surrender of Confederate general Robert E. Lee's Army of Northern Virginia signaled the beginning of the end of the Confederacy. President Lincoln immediately began thinking of all the work that needed to be done to reunite the country. He said to Gideon Welles, his secretary of the navy, "Civil government must be reestablished . . . as soon as possible. There must be courts, and law, and order, or society would be broken up."

On April 11, Lincoln stood on the White House balcony and delivered to the happy crowd that had gathered a carefully prepared speech on peace and Reconstruction. Lincoln stated that the Union would "mould from disorganized and discordant elements" new governments from the states that had seceded. He also publicly announced for the first time his desire for the enfranchisement of African Americans, which would give them the right to vote. Lincoln concluded by stating he would soon announce a new policy of restoration of those states to the Union.

One of the men in the crowd that day was actor John Wilkes Booth, a Southern sympathizer. When he heard Lincoln's statement about the African Americans, he said, "That means . . . citizenship. . . . That is the last speech he will ever make." Booth made good on his angry vow three days later on April 14, Good Friday. Lincoln and his wife were attending a play at Ford's Theater. Booth managed to sneak past the guards and into Lincoln's private box. There he pulled out a pistol and shot Lincoln in the head, mortally wounding him. Lincoln was carried to a boardinghouse across the street from the theater, where he died the next day.

Booth, meanwhile, escaped. He was found hiding in a barn on a farm in northern Virginia on April 26. Booth was shot and killed while trying to get away. An investigation revealed that Booth was one member in a conspiracy to assassinate the president, in part because of a belief that Lincoln was a tyrant who would impose harsh laws in the South. Unfortunately, by killing Lincoln, the conspirators removed the only man with sufficient power, prestige, and political skills who could stop the extreme members of the Republican Party—the radicals—from imposing the very laws and strict conditions the conspirators feared.

Opposite: The execution by hanging of four conspirators convicted of the assassination of President Lincoln.

ANDREW JOHNSON AND PRESIDENTIAL RECONSTRUCTION

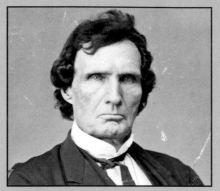

Above: Thaddeus Stevens was born poor, with a clubfoot and a childhood disease that left him bald. He wore a red wig for the rest of his life.

QUICK FACTS

☆ Unlike Lincoln, Johnson was a racist. In 1847, he said in Congress that African Americans were "inferior to the white man in point of intellect—better calculated in physical structure to undergo drudgery and hardship...." Because he believed that African Americans were inferior to whites, he blocked many attempts by Congress to establish racial equality for the former slaves.

☆ After Johnson was inaugurated, the office of vice president remained vacant during his administration. At the time, according to the Constitution, the person next in the line of succession for the presidency was the president pro tem of the Senate, Benjamin F. Wade.

Andrew Johnson, like Lincoln, was a self-made man of humble background. He became a member of the Democratic Party and held a number of state offices, including governor; he also served as a U.S. congressman and senator. When Tennessee seceded, Johnson remained with the Union, the only senator from a seceded state to do so. In gratitude for his loyalty and as a symbol of the unity he wished to restore, the Republican Lincoln asked the Southern Democrat to be his vice president in the 1864 election.

After Lincoln's assassination, radical Republicans were initially thrilled when Johnson became president. But Johnson, like Lincoln, believed that Reconstruction was primarily a job for the president, not Congress. Johnson also shared Lincoln's belief that the rebellion had been caused by individuals, not states. Although the individuals who led the rebellion might be punished, the states had always retained their constitutional rights.

On May 29, 1865, President Johnson issued two proclamations. The first offered amnesty and the restitution of property, except slaves, to most former Confederates who would take an oath of allegiance. Johnson's second proclamation replaced the Confederate governor of North Carolina with a provisional governor and directed him to call an election of delegates to create a new state constitution. Johnson shortly thereafter issued similar proclamations for six other Southern states. He also recognized the Lincoln-sponsored governments of Louisiana, Arkansas, and Tennessee. Johnson's minimum conditions for the new constitutions were: the abolition of slavery and the nullification of secession. As for individuals, banks, or countries that had loaned money to Confederate state governments, Johnson said those debts had to be cancelled and never repaid.

A few Republicans, led by Representative Thaddeus Stevens of Pennsylvania, claimed that Johnson's policy, which did not include giving the right to vote (to enfranchise) to freed slaves, was too lenient. However, more moderate Republicans were willing to give President Johnson's policy a chance. One said that if Southern states did not voluntarily enfranchise freedmen, the president "will then be at liberty to pursue a sterner policy." Unfortunately, Johnson and Congress would soon find themselves on a collision course that would threaten to topple the presidency.

Opposite: President Andrew Johnson.

"CONTRABANDS" AND FREEDMEN

Above: The Reliable Contraband illustrated the assistance freed slaves gave to the Union troops.

QUICK FACTS

⭐ The federal government paid contrabands working for the Union troops 25 cents a day plus food. Before 1864, a Union private received $13 a month and a $3-per-month clothing allowance. After 1864, he received $16 a month plus the clothing allowance. Before 1864, African-American troops received $10 a month, and after that their pay was equal to that of white troops.

⭐ The federal agency officially responsible for freedmen was created on March 3, 1865 and called the Bureau of Refugees, Freedmen, and Abandoned Lands, also known as the Freedman's Bureau. Because postwar conditions in the South were so bad, the Bureau assisted both black and white Southerners.

Until the Constitution could be amended to abolish slavery, the legal status of slaves in Southern territories captured by Union troops was unclear. General Benjamin Butler was the first Union general to take the initiative on this matter. Union forces had captured Fortress Monroe along the Virginia coast in 1861. Confederate fortifications surrounded the Union outpost, which was supplied and supported from the sea. In May of that year, three slaves, who were working on those fortifications, escaped to Butler's lines. The following day, under a flag of truce, the slaves' owner, a Confederate colonel, approached the Union lines. He demanded the return of his property, stating that, according to the terms of the federal Fugitive Slave Law that had been passed before the war, the Union troops were obligated to do so. Butler rejected the colonel's claim, stating the because Virginia said it was no longer in the Union, the law did not apply. Butler further said that, as property, slaves were subject to seizure as "contraband of war," in the same way as houses, wagons, horses, or livestock. Northern newspapers repeated this phrase, and shortly thereafter the word "contrabands" was used to describe slaves who escaped into Union lines. When the Thirteenth Amendment, which abolished slavery, became law in 1865, both contrabands and slaves had a new name: freedmen.

This was the first great step for the former slaves, but now the larger one lay ahead: helping the freedmen become productive citizens. When Lincoln made his proclamation of amnesty and Reconstruction in late 1863, he also recognized the responsibility due the former slaves. He said, "Any provision which may be adopted . . . in relation to freed people [by new state governments in the South] which shall recognize and declare their permanent freedom, provide for their education, and which may yet be consistent, as a temporary arrangement, with their present condition as a laboring, landless, and homeless class, will not be objected to by the national Executive."

Lincoln's proclamation could not settle all the issues regarding the freedmen's future, but it opened the door for private organizations to help. The American Missionary Association, the National Freedman's Relief Association, and others stepped in and assisted state, local, and military administrations in implementing a revolutionary social program whose purpose was nothing less than a wholesale transformation of the lives of four million people—approximately 12 percent of the nation's population.

Opposite: Fugitive African-American slaves in 1862, fording the Rappahannock River in Virginia in order to reach Union lines and freedom.

CARPETBAGGERS AND SCALAWAGS

Above: A political cartoon depicting the crushing burden carpetbagger rule had on the South.

QUICK FACTS

⭐ Many scalawags came from upland counties in eastern Tennessee; western North Carolina and Virginia; and northern Georgia, Alabama, and Arkansas. These were regions where slavery was not as common as elsewhere in the South and whose people had resented the plantation regime that had dominated government and the economy in the South prior to 1865.

⭐ At a time when fewer than 2 percent of the population were college graduates, many carpetbaggers had college degrees, making them one of the most educated groups in the United States.

The North's invasion of the South during the Civil War caused widespread destruction of land and property. At the end of the war, many regions in the South were in a state of anarchy. The collapse of Confederate authority left large areas without any government. Roaming groups of bandits plundered abandoned or defenseless homes. Hundreds of thousands of freed people and white refugees suffered from disease, exposure, and hunger. The Union army was the main source of enforcing law and order when it was in a particular region, but when it moved on, the task of administering the conquered territory had to be filled by other individuals. Resentful Southerners called these Northerners and Southerners who governed the regions "carpetbaggers" and "scalawags."

"Carpetbaggers" and "scalawags" are among the most hated words in American politics, particularly in the South. Carpetbaggers got their name from the thick, heavy cloth luggage they used to carry their clothing and other possessions. Most carpetbaggers were Union army officers who, upon their discharge, stayed in the South after the war. Southerners who hated them described the men as "gangs of itinerant adventurers, vagrant interlopers [that were] . . . depraved, dissolute, dishonest, and degraded. . . ." Though it is true that some were unscrupulous and opportunistic, wanting to enrich themselves at the expense of the South, most were not.

Scalawags were white Southerners who joined the Republican Party and received government and administrative jobs. They were resented by other Southerners who felt that they had become traitors or had sold out to the government in order to enrich themselves at their neighbor's expense. Southern Democrats called them "vile, blatant, vindictive, unprincipled . . . the mean, lousy, and filthy kind that are not fit for butchers or dogs." The term "scalawag" supposedly came from Scalloway, a tiny Scottish island noted for its scrubby cattle and horses.

Despite this overwhelming hatred and scorn, most carpetbaggers and scalawags proved to be men of great bravery and idealism, who possessed the courage of their convictions to promote necessary social changes and administer their duties as fairly as possible.

Opposite: Carpetbaggers by N. C. Wyeth depicts the enduring impression most people have of the people who came from the North to govern the South after the end of the war.

Above: The hides of more than forty thousand buffalo being prepared for shipment.

QUICK FACTS

⭐ Sea travel from New York to California was not easy. The shortest route was over the Isthmus of Panama. Because the Panama Canal did not exist, people had to leave ships harbored on the eastern side of the isthmus, trek over land, and board ships on the western side that would continue the route to California. This route took 5 weeks and was approximately 5,450 miles long. The other water route, around Cape Horn, the southernmost tip of South America, was 13,600 miles long and took 6 months.

⭐ Construction on other transcontinental railroads soon followed the completion of the first one. By 1900 the lines included the Northern Pacific in the north, and the Southern Pacific, and Atlantic and Pacific lines in the south.

The work of unifying the United States was not confined to the South and Reconstruction. Though the states of California, Oregon, and Nevada were a part of the Union, they were separated from the rest of the nation by more than one thousand miles of rugged land. Before 1869, the most efficient overland way to travel to the West was by stagecoach. It took about two weeks, and the trip was a bone-jarring test of endurance. Paved roads didn't exist. Instead the stagecoaches traveled on dirt trails that were rugged, rutted, and sometimes washed out by rain or flash floods. The coaches were often overcrowded, which added to the discomfort. A trip by sea was more comfortable, but that took months. The only practical answer for providing inexpensive and efficient movement of large amounts of goods and people was by railroad.

People had dreamed and planned about a railroad traversing the country for years, but such an effort was enormously expensive. Only the federal government had the kind of money needed to build one. On July 1, 1862, President Lincoln signed the Pacific Railway Act into law. This provided the money and means to get construction started. Though some track was laid, real construction had to wait until after the Civil War ended.

Two companies built the first transcontinental railroad. The Central Pacific Railroad started in California and worked its way east. The Union Pacific Railroad started in Nebraska and worked its way west. The government also gave the companies grants of land for each mile of railroad track laid. Construction of the railroad became a competition between the two companies that captured the nation's imagination. The *Omaha Weekly Herald* predicted, "American genius, American industry, American perseverance can accomplish almost anything." It would also take a lot of hard work from thousands of laborers.

The Union Pacific had the easier route because it was laying track over the prairie. Also, it had a large group of readily available laborers, including men recently discharged from the Union army and out of work ex-Confederate soldiers. The Central Pacific had to bore and blast its way through two mountain ranges—Sierra Nevada and the Rockies. It suffered from a labor shortage as well, because at that time California and Oregon were very thinly populated.

Charles Crocker, one of the owners of the Central Pacific, estimated that he needed ten thousand workers. He had fewer than six hundred. In desperation he asked his superintendent of construction, James Strobridge,

Opposite: The meeting of the Union Pacific and Central Pacific railroads at Promontory Point, Utah, on May 10, 1869.

Above: A Union Pacific advertisement.

QUICK FACTS

★ The railroad was the biggest reason that the buffalo all but vanished from the prairie. Railroad crews needed food, so the companies hired buffalo hunters to help feed them. The railroads also carried thousands of hunters from the East who wanted to shoot buffalo. Finally, buffalo-hide coats became fashionable. The slaughter was so great that by 1900, the buffalo was almost extinct.

★ One of the spikes from the joining ceremony was engraved with the words "May God continue the unity of our country as this railroad unites the two great oceans of the world."

to hire some local Chinese men. They had arrived from China with the hope of striking it rich in the California gold fields. Instead of striking it rich, like many others, they were struggling to make a living. Strobridge, reflecting the prejudice against the Chinese that was prevalent then, claimed they were too small, too weak, too frail, and that they could never be trained. Crocker convinced Strobridge to give some a try. They did so well that Crocker, noting that it was cheaper to bring workers by ship across the Pacific Ocean instead of overland, sent ships to China to import more. Strobridge overcame his prejudice and later said they were "the best in the world." Not only did they work hard, they also worked for less than white laborers. Before long, 90 percent of the Central Pacific's work force was Chinese.

One time, though, Crocker's faith in the Chinese wavered. The Summit Tunnel in the Sierra Nevada had to be cut through 1,659 feet of solid granite. Chinese laborers worked around the clock in shifts. The average progress in the twenty-foot-diameter tunnel was between six and twelve inches per twenty-four hours. Dismayed over the slow progress, Crocker hired Cornish miners working in Virginia City, Nevada, to begin work at the opposite side of the mountain. He thought they could make more progress than the Chinese, but he later recalled, "The Chinese, without fail . . . cut more rock in a week than the Cornish miners did." The Cornish men became disgusted and soon quit.

On May 10, 1869, at Promontory Point, Utah, the two lines officially met. Leland Stanford of the Central Pacific and Thomas Durant of the Union Pacific participated in a special ceremony. A silver hammer was used to drive in a ceremonial "last" spike made of gold to complete the line. When the last blow fell, a telegraph operator tapped the telegraph key, sending the word the nation was waiting to hear: DONE!

Grenville Dodge, chief engineer of the Union Pacific, later telegraphed Secretary of War John A. Rawlins, "The great work, commenced during the Administration of Lincoln, in the middle of great rebellion, is completed under Grant, who conquered the peace."

Opposite: An illustration of angry Cheyenne Indians destroying a section of railroad track.

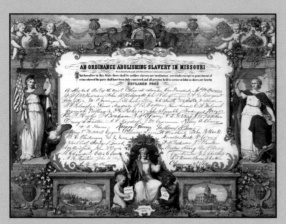

Above: A print of the *Emancipation Ordinance of Missouri* that officially abolished slavery in the state.

QUICK FACTS

☆ Seceded states had to ratify the Thirteenth Amendment as part of the conditions for their restoration into the Union.

☆ Susan B. Anthony decided to put the Fifteenth Amendment to a test. On November 1, 1872, Anthony and fifteen other women registered to vote in Rochester, New York. They voted on November 5, 1872. Less than a month later, on Thanksgiving Day, a deputy marshal came to her house with an arrest warrant. The warrant claimed she had broken an act of Congress. Anthony and the registrars were put to trial in June 1873. They were found guilty because the judge told the jurors, "I direct that you find a verdict of guilty."

The U.S. Constitution, the highest law in the nation, allows for changes, or amendments, to be added to it. The process of ratifying, or making an amendment into law, is not easy. First, two-thirds of Congress must approve the measure, and then the proposed amendment is presented to the states for voting. Only after three-fourths of the states vote in favor of the amendment does it finally become law.

The Thirteenth, Fourteenth, and Fifteenth Amendments are called the Civil War Amendments, because they dealt with important issues that were among the causes of the Civil War. The Thirteenth, ratified in 1865, abolished slavery. The Fourteenth, ratified in 1868, established individual rights and recognized racial equality. The Fifteenth, ratified in 1870, granted adult African-American males the right to vote.

The passage of the Thirteenth Amendment in Congress took a lot of work. Lincoln had done as much as he could as president, with his Emancipation Proclamation, to pave the way for the amendment. He used the considerable power of his personality and the office of the presidency to convince Congress to pass the amendment, which the House did on January 31, 1865. With the sentence "Neither slavery nor involuntary servitude . . . shall exist within the United States, or any place subject to their jurisdiction," the Thirteenth Amendment ended once and for all the legality of bondage of one person by another.

Unfortunately the grant of freedom and equality to African Americans emphasized the injustice under which American women, black and white, still lived. At the time women did not have the right to vote, and in some states they were not allowed to own property, have bank accounts, or any of the other things we take for granted today. When the Fifteenth Amendment was being debated, Elizabeth Cady Stanton and Susan B. Anthony, the founders of the National Women Suffrage Association, pushed to include the enfranchisement of women in the amendment. However, conservative prejudices against the idea of women voting were too strong to overcome. It would not be until the Nineteenth Amendment was ratified in 1920 that women would finally get the nationwide right to vote.

Opposite: A group of freedmen who were once the slaves of Confederate general Thomas F. Drayton.

LAND AND SOCIAL REFORM IN THE SOUTH

Above: A sharecropper's children in front of their home on an Alabama plantation.

QUICK FACTS

☆ Some freedmen became "sharecroppers." The landowner would give the freedman a portion of land where they could live and farm. In return, they had to share a portion of the crop's harvest with the landowner.

☆ Congressman Stevens proposed the confiscation of land owned by wealthy ex-Confederates and the allocation of 40-acre parcels of the land to each adult freedman. In fiery rhetoric that was typical of the time, he also said, "Strip a proud nobility of their bloated estates, . . . send them forth to labor, and teach their children to enter the workshop or handle the plow, and you will humble the proud traitors."

The abolition of slavery, brought about by the ratification of the Thirteenth Amendment in December 1865, made official the enormous social change in the South. Now black plantation workers would have to be paid for their labor. More important, they were free to leave the places where they had lived as slaves. The desire to move elsewhere was a powerful one. As one black preacher told his flock, "You ain't, non o' you, [going to] feel real free till you shakes the dust of the Ole Plantashun offen your feet an' goes to a new place where you can live out of sight of the great house."

Many freed people did leave the plantations—to search for relatives who years earlier had been sold to other slaveholders, to accept offers of higher wages elsewhere, or to move into cities where greater opportunity existed. Many others believed that only the ownership of land could make their freedom real. A black army veteran said, "Every colored man will be a slave, and feel himself a slave until he can raise [his] own bale of cotton and put [his] own mark upon it and say, '[This] is mine!'"

However, unless they received financial assistance of some kind, land ownership for freedmen was impossible. The only organization large enough to provide this level of assistance was the federal government. It moved rapidly to help. General William T. Sherman, the military governor in the southeast, issued his Special Field Orders, No. 15, which confiscated almost half a million acres of plantation lands in coastal Georgia and South Carolina that had been abandoned by planters during the war. This land, together with captured Confederate army horses, was turned over to the Freedmen's Bureau, which distributed the land and property in the South. The Freedmen's Bureau controlled nearly a million acres of abandoned and confiscated property which it distributed or leased to freedmen.

As a result of political battling between President Johnson and Congress, land reform did not become a part of Reconstruction. Johnson vetoed congressional land-reform bills, and ordered most of the confiscated land returned to the original owners upon their return. A majority of the freedmen did not achieve the economic independence for which they had hoped. Instead, they had to work for white landowners, who in many cases were their former masters.

Opposite: An 1870 photograph of a cotton harvest at a Southern plantation.

Above: A pioneer homestead with a sod house.

QUICK FACTS

⭐ Natural disasters, such as hailstorms and tornadoes, were—and still are—a constant threat to a farmer's livelihood in the Great Plains. One of the worst incidents occurred in the summer of 1874 when a plague of grasshoppers swept the prairie, consuming crops. Areas that they had ravaged were virtually stripped of vegetation.

⭐ A theory called "rain follows the plow" became popular in the late 1800s. Many farmers tilling prairie soil that had never been plowed believed that, by exposing moisture in the ground to the air, they caused the abundant rainfall that fell in the normally dry region during the 1870s and 1880s. Belief in this theory ended in the 1890s when a series of severe droughts hit the area.

The region of the Great Plains, which lies east of the Rocky Mountains, was called the "Great American Desert" by settlers going West. The Great Plains was flat—or nearly so—treeless, dry, wind-swept, and prone to extremes of temperature and weather conditions. In the summer the temperature could reach 110 degrees and in the winter drop to 40 degrees below zero.

Settlers who began staking their claims to land in the Great Plains were called "sodbusters" because of the cutting and turning action of their animal-drawn plows that tilled the soil. With the exception of patches of trees beside a river or a lake, wood was nonexistent. Settlers had to find other sources for shelter and fuel. Buildings were made from blocks of sod. Nicknamed "soddie," the structure was sturdy, cool in the summer, and warm in the winter, but there were disadvantages. Sod roofs leaked during rainstorms and shed dirt particles when dry.

Work on the frontier farms was hard, nonstop, and seemed to carry with it an endless variety of challenges. Livestock had to be fed, milked, let to pasture, watered, rounded up, and, occasionally, slaughtered. In the spring there was the plowing and planting; in the fall the harvesting. Throughout the year there was maintenance and repair of equipment, machinery, house, and outbuildings. Every member of the family, even the very youngest, helped.

Joseph Reed, a Kansas farmer, proudly wrote of his son, "Little Baz can run all over, fetch up cows out of the stock fields, or oxen, carry in stove wood and climb in the corn crib and feed the hogs and go on errands down at his grandma's." Baz was two years old.

The Reed farm was lucky to be in a region where sufficient trees existed for firewood. In most of the Great Plains, dried buffalo manure, called "buffalo chips," were gathered and used for fuel.

Lack of wood meant there were no wooden rails to fence in property. Not until 1873 was a practical and economic fence for the prairie developed: barbed wire. Invented by Illinois farmer Joseph F. Glidden, barbed wire revolutionized prairie life. Now farmers could protect their crops from foraging herds of cattle and buffalo.

Opposite: Nebraska homesteaders in the 1880s.

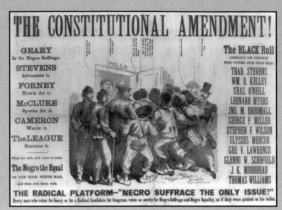

Above: A racist poster during the 1866 Pennsylvania gubernatorial campaign promoting the white-supremacy platform of Democratic candidate Hiester Clymer.

QUICK FACTS

☆ During the period of congressional Reconstruction 16 African Americans were elected to Congress. More than 600 held a variety of state offices in the South, and hundreds more were elected to local offices.

☆ The Reconstruction Act of 1867 was the first move by Congress to give itself complete military control of the region, in effect seizing for itself the commander-in-chief authority the Constitution gave the president.

☆ The Reconstruction Acts opened a period called "Black Reconstruction" in the South, which lasted from 1868–1877. It received its name from the large numbers of African Americans who served in the Southern state governments along with radical Republican officeholders.

The struggle between President Johnson and Congress over readmission of the seceded states became increasingly bitter. Because most of the Southern states did not have any representation in the federal government, they were largely spectators in the political war to decide their fate. Control of Reconstruction policies began to shift in Congress's favor with the election of 1866, which saw the Republicans retain their two-thirds majority in both houses. Exasperated by Southern states' rejection of the Fourteenth Amendment, in some cases with the active support of President Johnson, even the moderate legislators recognized that the only way that Reconstruction could advance was if they took action. As one moderate Republican said, "[The South] would not cooperate in rebuilding what they destroyed. . . . We must remove the rubbish and rebuild from the bottom."

The result was the Reconstruction Act of 1867. It divided the ten unreconstructed states—that is, all the former Confederate states except Tennessee, which had been readmitted to Congress because it had already ratified the Fourteenth Amendment—into five military districts. The act declared the existing civil governments temporary. It placed the states under military rule until such time as civil governments acceptable to Congress were formed. The act also set qualifications for voting rights designed to limit the power of the old Southern aristocracy. On March 2, 1867, President Johnson vetoed the bill. Later that day, both the House and Senate successfully voted to override the veto.

Despite this victory, some legislators had misgivings about whether or not this bill would be enough to change the political power base in the South. Congress soon passed a second Reconstruction Act that spelled out a process for Southerners to restore congressional representation for their states. The military governors were given the power to create state constitutional conventions. Recognizing that some white Southerners might try to intimidate freedmen, the voting rights of freedmen were ordered protected, and freedmen were granted the right to become elected representatives to the conventions. Congress also passed the Tenure of Office Act. It was specifically designed to limit the president's power to fire federally appointed employees, including cabinet officers, and was passed over President Johnson's veto. That act set the stage for the greatest post–Civil War drama in the nineteenth century: the impeachment of President Johnson.

Opposite: Senator Hiram R. Revels of Mississippi was the first African-American member of Congress.

Above: An impeachment trial pass to the press gallery.

QUICK FACTS

★ Thaddeus Stevens was sick when the impeachment trial began. He was too ill to deliver his closing arguments for impeachment and had to have it read for him. Stevens died shortly after the trial's conclusion.

★ One of the ironies of Johnson's impeachment trial was that it occurred in the last year of his term as president. It was obvious to everyone that he would never be nominated for reelection, but he had made so many bitter enemies that they refused to allow him the chance to leave quietly.

★ After he left the presidency, Johnson became one of the few presidents to return to political office. He was elected in 1875 to represent Tennessee in the Senate, but he died a few months after taking office.

Though Congress could dominate Reconstruction policies by overriding President Johnson's vetoes, it could not eliminate his ability to influence or block their enforcement. As a result, a growing number of radical Republicans decided that the only way Reconstruction could continue was to remove Johnson from office. In 1866 they proposed something that was unprecedented: impeachment.

Some moderates were disturbed by this action. Impeachment is a serious action. According to the Constitution, an officeholder can be impeached for "Treason, Bribery, or other High Crimes and Misdemeanors." First, the House must vote on whether or not there are grounds for impeachment. If the House votes that there are, then the Senate conducts a trial. Though the moderates hated Johnson's actions, they did not believe he had committed a crime. The radicals took the position that Johnson had misused his power and thus created a situation that harmed the public's welfare. Their first attempt to impeach Johnson was made in January 1867. Though that motion didn't succeed, the issue was not dead.

Seven months later, Johnson appeared to give the radicals the excuse they needed. On August 12, 1867, in an apparent violation of the Tenure of Office Act, Johnson suspended Secretary of War Edwin Stanton and, soon afterward, military governors Generals Philip Sheridan and Daniel Sickles. The Senate reinstated Stanton. Johnson then dismissed him, bringing on the impeachment vote.

The trial captured the attention of the nation. Some feared a rebel resurgence in the South if Johnson were convicted. Others distrusted the man who would succeed Johnson, radical Senator Wade, the president pro tem of the Senate. Still others were afraid that government system of checks and balances would be toppled in favor of Congress.

On May 16, 1868, the Senate trial ended and the vote was taken. A two-thirds majority was necessary for conviction. The roll call proceeded alphabetically. When Republican senator Peter G. Van Winkle from West Virginia voted for acquittal, impeachment had fallen one vote short. Technically, Johnson had won. Though he remained in office, he had lost the ability to influence government. Even so, the office of the president of the United States had survived its greatest challenge.

Opposite: An illustration of the chamber of the U.S. Senate during the impeachment trial of President Johnson.

PRESIDENT ULYSSES S. GRANT

Above: A sign from Grant's presidential bid.

QUICK FACTS

★ Ulysses S. Grant was not his original name. When Grant was born, he was christened Hiram Ulysses Grant. While a boy, he called himself Ulysses, because he wanted to avoid initials that spelled "H.U.G." When he arrived at West Point, a clerical error listed him as Ulysses S. Grant, which he decided to adopt.

★ After the presidency, Grant suffered a number of financial disasters that left him bankrupt. He accepted an offer by the author Samuel Clemens to publish his memoirs. While writing, Grant was revealed to have had terminal cancer of the throat. Grant died 8 days after finishing the project. His *Personal Memoirs* would become a bestseller.

★ Though Grant was famous for his military skill, he wrote, "The truth is I am more of a farmer than a soldier. . . . I never went into the army without regret and never retired without pleasure."

Ulysses S. Grant's life was one of the more remarkable success stories in America. He was the son of a farmer and small businessman. He attended West Point, which he later called "the most beautiful place I have ever seen." He also noted, "If a man graduates here, he is safe for life, let him go where he will." For Grant that path led him to Mexico in the U.S.-Mexican War (1847–1848) when he distinguished himself. After the war he was posted to the frontier of California, far from his wife and family. Forced to resign from the army for drunkenness in 1854, Grant struggled at a variety of jobs from farming, to selling cordwood, to being a real-estate agent. When the Civil War broke out, Grant volunteered for service in the Union army and was appointed a colonel of the Twenty-first Illinois Volunteers in June 1861. That was the start of a military career of extraordinary success that would be highlighted by his appointment as commander in chief of the Union armies. At the end of the war in 1865, Grant was the Union's most famous and powerful general.

As early as 1867 it became obvious to many political experts that General Ulysses S. Grant would be the Republican nominee for president of the United States in the 1868 campaign. The early predictions became fact when Grant was unanimously nominated to be the party's candidate in May 1868. His Democratic challenger was a former governor of New York, Horatio Seymour.

The Democrats' campaign was combative and racist. In contrast, the Republicans repeated Grant's last sentence in his letter accepting the nomination in speeches throughout the country, "Let us have peace." To voters weary from four years of military war and three years of political struggle over Reconstruction, Grant's statement struck a responsive chord.

When the November election concluded, Grant was declared the winner. The Republicans won overwhelmingly in Congress as well, retaining a two-thirds majority in the House of Representatives and four-fifths in the Senate.

With solid control of the legislature and with Andrew Johnson gone, it would appear that the Republicans would have no problem continuing their policy of Reconstruction.

Opposite: President Grant was reelected to a second term. Here he is taking the oath of office on March 4, 1873.

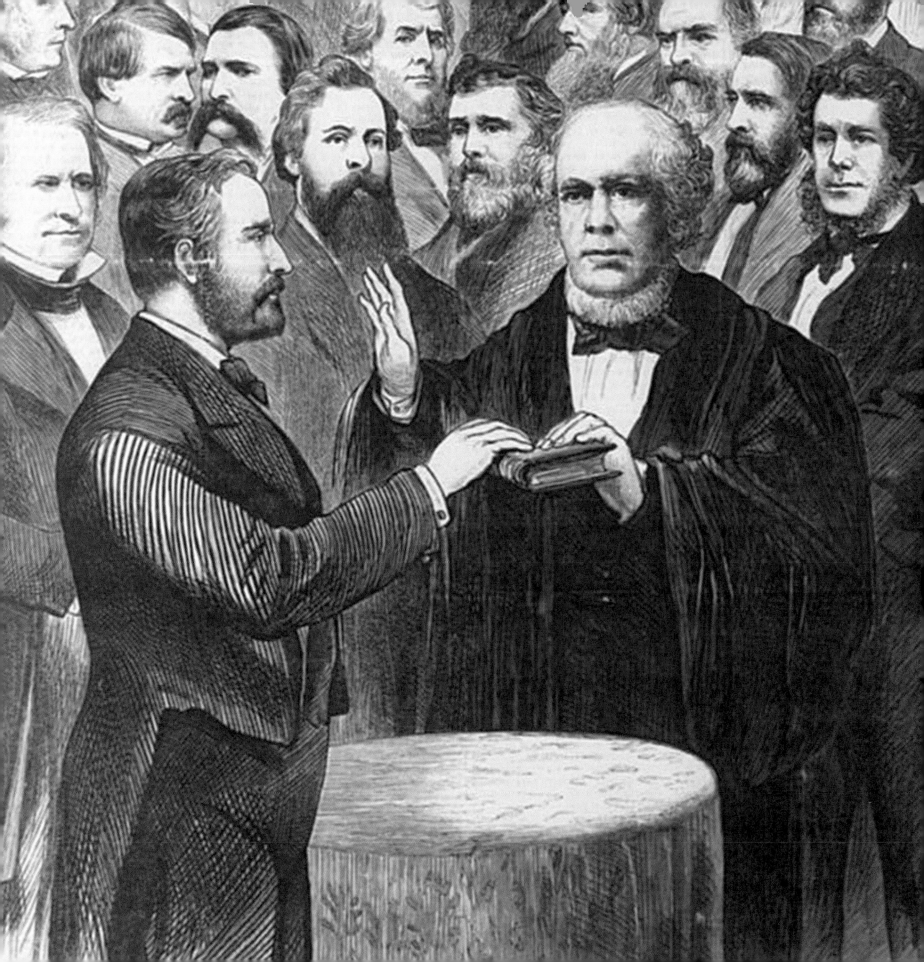

CORRUPTION, SCANDAL, AND THE CIVIL SERVICE

Above: Schuyler Colfax, vice president during Grant's first term.

QUICK FACTS

⭐ The period of economic boom following the Civil War was called the "Gilded Age," after a book by Mark Twain and Charles Dudley Warner, which condemned the way many unscrupulous men got rich through the unfair manipulation of the stock market, monopolies, and bribery to politicians.

⭐ Another disgrace during the Grant administration was the Crédit Mobilier scandal. It involved the illegal transfer of federal money that was supposed to go to railroad construction but went into the pockets of the company's owners instead. It also involved briberies to many powerful politicians. When the scandal broke, a newspaper published a list of all the congressmen and senators who received bribes, as well as Schuyler Colfax, Grant's vice president during his first term, and Henry Wilson, the vice president in Grant's second term.

Both political parties during this period practiced a patronage system that rewarded loyal party members with government jobs. The lure of such rewards insured party loyalty during the periods when the party was out of power. And when in power, the party assessed a "tax" of 2 or 3 percent of the officeholder's salary in order to provide money for political campaigns.

The president of the United States, as chief executive of the federal government, was at the top of the heap when it came to the number of government jobs he could hand out. When Grant won the election in 1868, he was besieged by job seekers to a point that he complained, "Patronage is the bane of the Presidential office. There is no man so anxious for civil service reform as the President. . . . He is necessarily a civil service reformer because he wants peace of mind." In December 1870, in the president's annual message to Congress, Grant urged reform legislation.

However, reformers became disillusioned with Grant, because they felt his words were not backed by appropriate actions. Grant's cabinet was primarily composed of his friends. Grant was an honest man, but a poor judge of character. He trusted people to a fault. This was a period of history marked by explosive growth when everyone was out to get rich quick in one way or another. As a result, during the eight years he was president, his administration was wracked by scandal, including accusations against the attorney general's wife and the secretary of the interior's son for accepting bribes to influence government policy, and the notorious Whisky Ring scandal in which distillers bribed federal revenue agents and other government officials and cheated the government out of millions of tax dollars.

Grant succeeded in creating the U.S. Civil Service Commission in 1872. The commission recommended competitive examinations for various nonelective government offices. It also urged the abolition of the party taxes on salaries. Because Congress refused to give it a meaningful budget for enforcement, it was largely ineffective. It would not be until the early twentieth century that true civil service reform would happen.

Opposite: A political cartoon satirizing President Grant and the scandals in his administration.

Above: Immigrants on the
S. S. *Patricia* in New York Harbor.

QUICK FACTS

⭐ Most immigrants became assimilated in their new country to the extent that the third generation was clearly American, but evidence of their cultural heritage remains in local festivals and in the names of cities, including Bismarck, North Dakota, (from German settlers) and Dagmar, Montana (settled by Danes).

⭐ Some immigrants went west to strike it rich as miners. Those who came after the Civil War discovered that the best California gold fields and the Nevada silver mines were either taken or stripped of ore. Tales of new gold strikes, such as near Pike's Peak in Colorado and in the Black Hills of Dakota Territory (now South Dakota), would lure some to those regions. But most miners wound up digging out ore as laborers for the large mining companies.

With the expansion to the West, the government and the railroad companies had land, but they still needed people to settle it. The first group that came was comprised of U.S. citizens from the East and South, all hoping to start a new life following the Civil War. However, this migration was merely a trickle in a territory that was larger than some European nations. What the government and the railroad companies needed was a flood of people. The generous terms of the Homestead Act of 1862, which offered ownership of 160 acres of land virtually for free, provided an incentive and was an important first step. The next step was getting the word out to people around the world.

Railroad agents went to Europe and advertised heavily, promoting the opportunity of a new life in the "wide open spaces." Frontier states and territories created immigration boards and also conducted their own promotional campaigns to lure immigrants. Agents would greet immigrant ships docking in New York City and pass out pamphlets and newspapers, which were printed in the immigrants' languages to promote opportunities available in their respective regions. They came, wanting a chance to live a new, better life, to own land, to escape religious or political persecution. They were citizens from Ireland, Italy, Germany, Norway, Sweden, Denmark and other countries. Some, such as the Czechs, German-Russians, and Poles, were ethnic groups dominated by an unfriendly imperial power. Still others, including Jews and Mennonites, came seeking religious freedom.

From 1860 to 1900, more than twelve million Europeans entered the United States. Most settled in large cities and communities east of the Mississippi River. Many others, lured by the promises of the agents and by letters of relatives who had preceded them, settled throughout the West.

Because they spoke little or no English, most immigrants tended to settle in the same region, forming large ethnic groups within the state or territory; still the transition between their old life and new, particularly on the frontier, was immense. In Europe, most had lived in densely populated areas with better-developed roads, agriculture, strict class and social structures. They had been surrounded by forests, rivers, and mountains. In the American West, they were pioneers, where distances between settlements and even neighbors were often measured in miles, not feet. The sense of isolation and the feeling of insignificance were accented by the vast flatness of the Great Plains and the awesome celestial dome of the clear, night sky.

Opposite: Swedish pioneers in Park River, North Dakota, vicinity in 1888.

ROUGHING IT: WOMEN ON THE FRONTIER

Above: Calamity Jane, whose real name was Martha Jane Cannary Burke.

QUICK FACTS

⭐ Sarah Raymond was a young woman when she made the journey with her family to Virginia City in the Montana Territory in 1865. She wrote of the journey, "Oh, the dust, the dust; it is terrible. I have never seen it half as bad; it seems to be almost knee-deep in places."

⭐ Once a community was large enough, women would arrange to have a school established. Most of the teachers were women, and some as young as fifteen years old.

⭐ Two of the most common books in frontier homes were the family Bible and a wish book—a mail-order catalogue. An invention of businessman Montgomery Ward, these catalogues featured everything a person on the frontier needed: clothing, tools, seeds—in some you could even buy a house.

The decision to go West was almost always made by men. Many women would express in their diaries their resentment over the uprooting. Writer and artist Mary Anna Hallock Foote left her comfortable life in the East to live with her husband, Arthur, in a rough mining town in California where he dreamed of making his fortune. Her experiences were turned into a series of articles, and later novels, about life in the American West. She wrote, "When an Eastern woman goes West, she parts at one wrench with family, clan, traditions, clique, cult and all that hitherto enabled her to merge her outlines—the support, the explanation, the excuse, should she need one for her personality."

What to take and what to leave became two of many deeply personal decisions women had to make. As a result, such trivial items as combs, mirrors, and hair ribbons, as well as other necessarily small mementos—family photographs and even flower and shrub seeds from family gardens—assumed enormous emotional importance because of their connection to a past life and distant relatives and friends.

Childbearing on the frontier became a mixed blessing that bordered on torture, especially if it occurred while traveling on a wagon train, the usual method of migration west before the railroads were built. Because wagon masters were anxious to make it through the mountain passes before they were stopped by snow, unscheduled stops were rarely tolerated. A woman was considered fortunate if the wagon train halted for a day to allow her to give birth to her child. Also, it was rare for a doctor to be on the wagon train, so any medical assistance usually came from other women.

Yet, hand in hand with the hardship came the enhanced opportunities that were part and parcel of frontier life. The rugged way of life, with its sparse population and shared dangers, bred independence. The opportunity of working for pay in a variety of careers became available to women often because there simply weren't enough men to fill the positions.

Nannie Alderson traveled from her home in Union, West Virginia, in 1880 to visit her aunt in Atchison, Kansas. She wrote, "What impressed me most was the fact that a girl could work in an office or a store, yet that wouldn't keep her from being invited to the nicest homes or marrying one of the nicest boys. This freedom to work seemed to me a wonderful thing."

Opposite: A woman on the Oregon frontier with her baby in a makeshift crib.

WYOMING TERRITORY AND WOMEN'S SUFFRAGE

Above: A wooden jailhouse in Wyoming Territory.

QUICK FACTS

⭐ One of the first efforts toward women's suffrage occurred in 1848 when Eastern feminists gathered in Seneca Falls, New York, and issued a declaration of women's rights. On that list was the right to vote.

⭐ After 1869, women in Wyoming voted and participated in other civic duties, including jury duty. A few years later, Boston newspapers published a story by a "prominent gentlemen from Wyoming" who testified that women's suffrage had been a catastrophe in the Wyoming Territory. When someone telegraphed the mayor of Cheyenne seeking "the particulars concerning this prominent gentleman," he wired back, "A horse thief convicted by a jury, half of whom were women."

The frontier was a land of promise to women as well as men, but for all of their greater freedom, the one thing they shared with their sisters in the East was the fact that they did not have the right to vote. Mrs. Esther Hobart McQuigg Morris was determined to change that. Wyoming was still a territory in 1869 when fifty-five-year-old Mrs. Morris arrived from Illinois to be with her husband and two grown sons in the mining camp of South Pass City. Her mind was firmly set on getting women the right to vote, and she believed that her best opportunity was with a territorial government in the West. Territorial elections were scheduled for the fall of 1869, and the legislature would be taking up the issue of drafting a state constitution. Representatives of the state constitution convention would also decide who would be allowed to vote. As long as their rules did not violate the federal Constitution—for instance, as long as they did not forbid African Americans from voting—Wyoming and other territories were allowed to choose which of its citizens would be allowed to vote—including women. This was Mrs. Morris's chance, and she passionately went to work.

After his election to the Wyoming Territory legislature, William H. Bright, at the urging of Mrs. Morris, introduced a women's enfranchisement bill. The legislature approved it. Despite pressure from antisuffrage groups, the territorial governor signed the measure into law.

Wyoming petitioned Congress for statehood, and the issue came up for vote in 1890. Considerable controversy arose because the proposed state constitution contained a clause granting women the right to vote, something no other state in the Union had. A group of women telegraphed their representatives in Washington, D.C., and said that if that issue was the one item barring Wyoming from statehood, it should be deleted. They were sure of its renewal. The men of the Wyoming territorial legislature gallantly replied, "We will remain out of the Union a hundred years, rather than come in without women."

Wyoming became the forty-fourth state on July 10, 1890—the first state to grant women the right to vote. Esther Morris was among the honored guests participating in the ceremonies. She presented to the new state governor a forty-four-star flag made by the women of Wyoming.

Opposite: An illustration showing women voting in Cheyenne, Wyoming, in the presidential election of 1888.

Above: Senator Charles Sumner.

QUICK FACTS

⭐ By June 1868, every seceded state except Texas had met congressional standards and been readmitted to representation in Congress. Texas would not be readmitted until March 1870.

⭐ Blanche Bruce and Hiram Revels were two African Americans elected to the U.S. Senate from the state of Mississippi. Revels took the old seat of former Senator Jefferson Davis, who during the war was the president of the Confederate States of America.

⭐ Senator Sumner was a crusader for social issues for most of his government career. He first spoke out against slavery in 1852. In 1856, Senator Sumner delivered a speech denouncing slavery. In it he insulted South Carolina senator Andrew P. Butler. Two days later, Butler's nephew, South Carolina congressman Preston S. Brooks, angrily stormed into the Senate chamber and assaulted Senator Sumner with a cane.

As important as the Civil War Amendments were in ending slavery and establishing the citizenship and voting rights for African Americans, they did not solve all the post–Civil War issues that arose. Discrimination and segregation were widespread, mostly in the South, but in parts of the North as well. In 1866 the Republicans realized the need for additional legislation to guarantee the rights of African Americans.

Congress passed its first Civil Rights Act in 1866, over President Johnson's veto. Because Congress could not get the necessary two-thirds majority to override Johnson's veto, this first attempt did not become law.

However, the issue remained important to many federal legislators and Senator Charles Sumner in 1870 introduced a bill to prohibit racial discrimination in schools, juries, and all forms of transportation and public accommodations anywhere in the United States. The first time he introduced the bill, it was defeated, but he refused to give up. He said his goal was to "remove the last lingering taint of slavery" from the country. For the next four years, with each new session of Congress, he introduced his civil rights bill, and in 1871, 1872, and 1873, it was defeated.

Even the advocates of racial equality, the radical Republicans, were unsure about Sumner's measure. One radical Republican newspaper editor wrote that "It is far better to have both [races] educated, even in 'separate' schools, than not to have them educated at all." Sumner's civil rights bill was finally passed by the Senate in May 1874. The House of Representatives passed its version of the bill soon afterward. Sumner's bill became law in 1875, but he did not live to enjoy the victory. He had died in March 1874.

The Civil Rights Act of 1875 was a historic measure that proved to be years ahead of its time. Although some railroads, streetcar lines, and restaurants and theaters in the South and North served blacks on a nonsegregated basis after the passage of the law, most did not.

In 1883, the United States Supreme Court ruled the Civil Rights Act of 1875 to be unconstitutional, because while the Fourteenth Amendment gave Congress the power to legislate against state discrimination, that power did not extend to individuals or private companies.

Opposite: South Carolina congressman, Preston S. Brooks, attacking Senator Sumner on the Senate floor in 1856.

PREJUDICE, RACISM, AND THE KU KLUX KLAN

Above: A nineteenth-century political cartoon by Thomas Nast titled "The Union as it Was. The Lost Cause. Worse than Slavery" commenting about the prejudice and violence against African Americans following the Civil War.

QUICK FACTS

⭐ Nathan Bedford Forrest, one of the Confederacy's greatest cavalry generals, was one of the leaders of the Ku Klux Klan. In August 1868, he publicly warned Republican leaders in Tennessee not to call out troops to fight the Klan. He said that all the Republicans in Memphis were marked for death, "and if trouble should break out, none of them would be left alive."

⭐ Klan members covered their faces because they did not want to be identified. When they terrorized African Americans, some Klan members pretended to be the ghosts of Confederate soldiers.

A lost war and constitutional amendments did not mean all of white society would accept freed former slaves. Inevitably African Americans in the South became the targets and victims of anger and resentment by the defeated white Southerners, though racism also existed in the North. In the fall of 1865, three northern states, Connecticut, Wisconsin, and Minnesota, had state constitutional amendments on the ballot that would give African Americans the right to vote. In all three states, the amendments were defeated.

In the South, racist hatred and fear of black rule was a major issue. In the election of 1868, one conservative newspaper in North Carolina carried the large headline: "The Great and Paramount Issue is: Shall Negroes or White Men Rule North Carolina?" This issue galvanized some whites to form guerilla organizations whose purpose was to terrorize African Americans in order to keep them from voting. The most infamous of these groups was the Ku Klux Klan, whose members came from all social classes in the South.

Violence by the Klan and similar organizations became so severe that in 1871, Congress convened a special session and passed what was called the Ku Klux Klan Act on April 20, which declared such organizations illegal. One woman who testified at that session, Maria Carter, told of how forty or fifty Klansmen came to her home "My husband went to kindle a light, and they busted both doors open and ran in. . . . One put his gun down to him and said, 'Is this John Walthall?' They had been hunting him a long time. They had gone to my brother-in-law's hunting him, and had whipped one of my sisters-in-law powerfully and two more men on account of him."

After he signed the bill into law, President Grant and his administration moved swiftly to crack down on the racist organizations. In two years, from 1871–1872, thousands of suspected Klansmen and other racist group leaders were arrested. Violent racist incidents against African Americans soon dropped. Because the government's main purpose was to stop the violence against African Americans, rather than secure convictions, most of those arrested were eventually granted clemency, received presidential pardons, or received suspended sentences or fines after plea bargains. All who did receive jail sentences, even the most violent offenders, were freed by 1875.

Opposite: Two members of the Ku Klux Klan, 1868.

Above: President Hayes.

QUICK FACTS

☆ Hayes was a Civil War Union general and had served in various government positions, among them, governor of Ohio. He supported reform movements, including a civil service system based on merit rather than political influence, but he did not take the extreme views of the radicals. He was also a moderate on Southern policy.

☆ Organizations that did the most to help freedmen buy land were the freedmen's aid societies and the Freedman's Bank. The freedmen's aid societies bought land in the South and then resold it in small lots to freedmen. The Freedman's Bank was founded in 1865 and helped thousands of freedmen buy homes, farms, and businesses. At its peak it had 100,000 depositors and accounts totaling $57 million. The bank lost all its money in the economic depression known as the Panic of 1873 and was forced to close in 1874.

In 1874 Reconstruction had been in existence for a little more than ten years. During that time, slavery had been abolished and male African Americans had been given citizenship and the right to vote. However, many antebellum white Southern attitudes remained. Most white Southerners were not ready to accept as their mayor, governor, senator, or congressman someone who was once property that they had bought and sold. Though ten years is too short a time to change an attitude created by generations of social custom, in politics, ten years is an eternity.

Even during the war and its immediate aftermath, only the radical Republicans and a minority of like-minded whites in the North were fully committed to full racial equality. Most Northern voters were more concerned about local "pocketbook" issues, such as employment, the economy, and the cost of goods and services. For them, the plight of faraway blacks was largely a nonissue. An editorial in the *Washington National Republican* observed, "People are becoming tired of . . . abstract questions, in which the overwhelming majority of them have no direct interest. The negro question, with all its complications, and the reconstruction of the Southern States, with all its interminable embroilments, have lost much of the power they once wielded."

However, the largest blow to Reconstruction occurred following the presidential election of 1876 between Democrat Samuel Tilden and Republican Rutherford B. Hayes. It was a hard-fought battle. At first it appeared that Tilden had narrowly won, but the votes in three Southern states—South Carolina, Louisiana, and Florida—were contested. Accusations of fraud and voter intimidation in the three states forced Congress to create a special commission to examine the votes and decide the results. Their decision threw the election to Hayes. Needless to say it was a decision marked with controversy.

One of the many unsubstantiated charges leveled against Hayes was that he made a secret deal with Southern Democrats, promising to pull out all federal troops and end Reconstruction if they would concede in his favor. Unsubstantiated charges notwithstanding, after he was inaugurated in 1877, Hayes did order the federal troops out of the South, thus ending the last trace of military rule. Reconstruction was over.

Opposite: A lithograph depicting important African-American leaders both before and during Reconstruction. The group includes government officials, politicians, ministers, educators, diplomats, lawyers, and businessmen. In the center is abolitionist Frederick Douglass.

DISTINGUISHED COLORED MEN

Frederick Douglass
THE COLORED CHAMPION OF FREEDOM

THE COWBOY

Above: A cowboy with the tools of his trade: a wide-brimmed hat to shield against the sun, a bandana to protect his mouth and nose from dust, chaps to protect his legs, and a lariat for roping cattle.

QUICK FACTS

☆ The heyday of the cowboy lasted only 20 years, from 1865–1885. During that period approximately 40,000 cowboys rode the range.

☆ No one is certain of the origin of the word "cowboy." During the Revolutionary War, it described armed Tories who tinkled cowbells to ambush farmer-patriots, searching for lost cows. Later the word described Texas bandits, who stole cattle from the Mexicans. It may also have been derived from the Spanish word *vaquero*, which came from the Spanish word for "cow," *vaca*. Only after the Civil War did "cowboy" acquire its present meaning.

Not long after he arrived at Medora, Dakota Territory, future president Theodore Roosevelt, then in his late twenties, wrote to his friend Henry Cabot Lodge, saying, in part, "You would hardly know me. . . . [I feel] as absolutely free as a man could feel." Roosevelt had gone west from New York in 1884 following the double tragedy of the deaths of his mother (of typhoid fever) and his young wife (of Bright's disease, a disease of the kidneys). He hoped to overcome his sorrow through what he called "the strenuous life." Roosevelt, a Harvard-educated man from a socially prominent family, suffered from asthma and was almost blind without his glasses, but became a rancher and earned the respect of the rough and tumble men who worked for him—cowboys.

In legend the cowboy became one of the great icons of America. Sitting tall in the saddle; busting broncos; herding cattle; battling weather, hostile Native Americans, bandits, and cattle rustlers; and living life to the fullest against the spectacular backdrop of mountains, mesas, buttes, and rolling prairie of the free range—this romantic image continues to captivate our imagination today. In real life the cowboy was merely the hired hand of the rancher or cattle baron, who did everything necessary to operate the ranch or cattle drive. Cowboys were overworked, poorly paid laborers who sweated under the scorching sun or froze in the bitterly cold winters as they herded, branded, and tended cattle, repaired barns, outbuildings, and corrals, and did anything else the rancher or cattle baron required. Boredom and loneliness were constant companions. Danger came more often from tornadoes, lightning and snowstorms, flash floods, stampedes, and rattlesnakes than from Native Americans and outlaws. Still, they were men who epitomized the American spirit of freedom and independence in a frontier where a person could carve out a new life.

Cowboys also lived by an unwritten code of honorable conduct that Theodore Roosevelt admired. "Meanness, cowardice, and dishonesty are not tolerated," he observed. "There is a high regard for truthfulness and keeping one's word, intense contempt for any kind of hypocrisy, and a hearty dislike for a man who shirks his work."

Roosevelt arrived in the West as the frontier era was coming to an end. He counted himself lucky to be able to participate in a lifestyle he knew would soon vanish.

Opposite: Ranchers and cowboys in southwestern Colorado.

THE CATTLE DRIVES

Above: Cowboys eating out in front of a chuck wagon.

58

QUICK FACTS

⭐ The invention of refrigerated railroad cars in the 1870s made it possible for Chicago stockyards to ship fresh beef anywhere in the country.

⭐ Cattle brands were used to identify ownership of the cattle. Brands were formally registered and were usually formed from combinations of the letters of the alphabet. On the ranch, preschool-age children learned about the alphabet, because they often helped with the branding. As a result, they usually had the alphabet memorized before they were old enough to go to school.

⭐ Cattle rustling and rebranding was a common occurrence. One rancher who suffered from this problem had the brand "IC." A neighboring rancher who stole his cattle rebranded the cows so that the brand read "ICU." The first rancher round up these stolen head, had a new brand registered, and then had the recaptured cows branded "ICU2."

Cattle drives were among the most celebrated events of this period. Thousands of head of cattle from pastures in southern and central Texas were rounded up by cowboys and herded hundreds of miles north to railroad terminals in Kansas and elsewhere. The drives all originated near San Antonio, Texas, and generally followed one of four major routes to cities that had railroad terminals and stockyards large enough to accommodate the herds. The most famous trails were the Goodnight-Loving Trail, which ended at Cheyenne, Wyoming; the Western Trail, which went to Dodge City, Kansas; the Chisholm Trail, which went to both Ellsworth and Abilene, Kansas; and the Sedalia Trail, which angled east and ended at Sedalia, Missouri.

Owners of large ranches, who were called "cattle barons," could raise huge herds containing tens of thousands of cattle, because the animals could be fed for free on the vast tracts of government-owned frontier land. The dominant cattle breed in the region during this period was the Texas longhorn, so named because its horns were known to measure more than forty inches across from tip to tip. It was a hardy species brought by the Spanish explorers and settlers in the 1700s from the Andalusia region of Spain. It adapted well to the harsh conditions of the Texas frontier and for many years roamed wild. Even though its meat was of a lower quality than other breeds, the Texas longhorn dominated the beef market, because the cost of raising herds was so low.

The first great cattle drive, containing a herd of approximately 260,000 head, began in the spring of 1866. It was an eight-hundred-mile trip from San Antonio to Sedalia. The drive encountered such challenges and dangers as: disease, stampedes, bad weather, Indians, cattle rustlers, and angry farmers who saw their crops eaten and trampled. Even though only a few thousand of the original herd survived the drive to Sedalia, the high price the stock fetched convinced the ranchers that the system could work.

By 1867, the Kansas Pacific Railroad had extended as far west as Abeline, Kansas, reducing the trip from the south Texas ranches by 150 miles and allowing for a straight north drive through Indian Territory (modern Oklahoma). The first drive to Abeline reached the city in the summer of 1867, where approximately 35,000 longhorns were loaded onto cattle cars for the trip to the stockyards of Kansas City and Chicago. From 1867 to 1871, more than a million longhorns traveled the Chisholm Trail alone.

Opposite: Map of cattle drive trails.

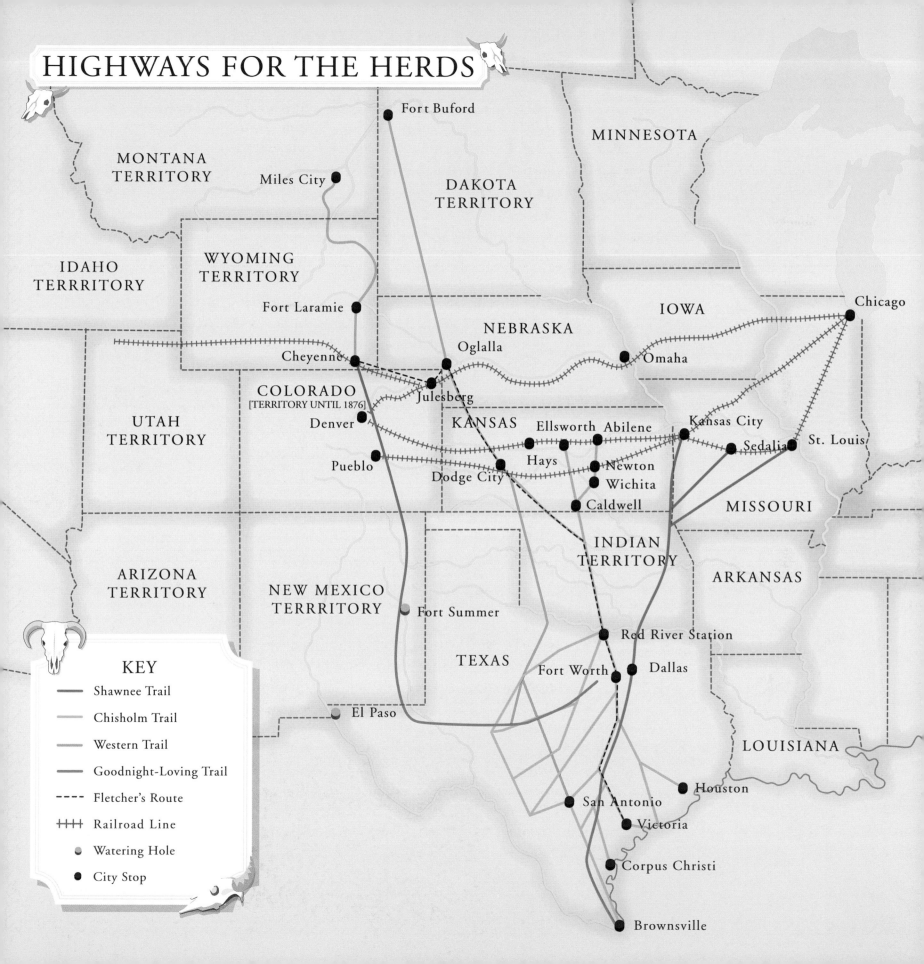

Above: A Sioux camp near Pine Ridge, South Dakota.

QUICK FACTS

⭐ One of the fundamental differences between the settlers of the United States and the Native Americans was the concept of land ownership. The tribes each lived and roamed on territory that they cherished as a birthright and held for common use by the whole tribe. The idea of a single individual having ownership of a unit of land, authorized by a piece of paper called a "deed," was incomprehensible.

⭐ The peak period of treaty signings was between 1853 and 1857, when 174 million acres throughout the West, an area larger than Texas, became the property of the United States government.

Westward expansion of white settlements in the frontier boomed, creating problems with the Indians already on the land, who resented the invasion of the white man. The government attempted to peacefully solve the problem with the reservation system. Reservations are territorial units, smaller than the original ancestral land, retained by Native American tribes through treaty and governed by tribal and federal rule.

A series of reservation treaties signed with the Plains tribes in the late 1860s and 1870s gave Indians exclusive use of the reservation land "for as long as the grass grows and the water flows." Limited by the shrunken borders of the reservation, they became dependent on federal Indian Agency goods and supplies. They also had to "learn the White Man's ways," and become settlers themselves, learning farming and trading skills.

However, as more and more white settlers entered the frontier, the federal government revised existing treaties, further reducing the size of Indian land. The most sweeping document affecting Native Americans was the General Allotment Act of 1887, also called the Dawes Severalty Act or just the Dawes Act. Sponsored by Massachusetts senator Henry L. Dawes, who idealistically hoped it would help assimilate Native Americans into white society, this landmark legislation dissolved the legal status of the tribe, offered them the opportunity to become U.S. citizens, and allotted each head of a family a "homestead" of 160 acres of farmland or 320 acres of grazing land. Other individuals in the tribe received allotments of eighty acres. Any reservation left after the allotments were distributed was declared "surplus land" that could then be sold. Ultimately the tribes lost a total of 108 million acres of land under the Dawes Act. Sioux Chief Red Cloud commented on his tribe's relationship with the whites over the years: "They made us many promises, more than I can remember, but they never kept but one; they promised to take our land, and they took it."

Losing so much land was hard for many Indians to accept. Those who resisted, such as Sioux Chiefs Sitting Bull and Crazy Horse, and their followers, were called "hostiles." Chief Satanta of the Kiowa tribe expressed the feelings of the hostile Indians when he said, "I love the land and the buffalo. I love to roam over the wide prairie, and when I do, I feel free and happy, but when we settle down we grow pale and die."

Opposite: Blackfeet braves.

THE OUTLAWS

Above: Townspeople hold up the bodies of the Dalton brothers after their failed robbery attempts on two banks in Coffeyville, Kansas.

QUICK FACTS

⭐ After the Daltons' failed bank robberies, townspeople took photos with the dead Bob Dalton and dying Grattan Dalton. One townsman pumped Grattan's arm up and down so that blood would spurt out of the bullet wound in his neck.

⭐ In 1899 outlaw Pearl Hart robbed a stagecoach in Arizona, thus earning a name for herself as the last stagecoach bandit in the West.

⭐ Billy the Kid's exploits were detailed in newspapers across the country. In 1880, he told a reporter from the *Las Vegas Gazette*: "I don't blame you for writing of me as you have. You had to believe other stories, but then I don't know if anyone would believe anything good of me anyway."

The outlaws—mostly men, but also some women—were among the most colorful characters to contribute to the American frontier's reputation as the "Wild West." Jesse and Frank James became legends whose fame endures to this day. They were originally members of Quantrill's Raiders, the Confederate guerilla group that fought the Union during the Civil War. After the war, they teamed with the Younger brothers, Cole, Jim, Bob, and John. From 1866–1876, the James-Younger gang "earned" a living robbing banks, stores, stagecoaches, and trains.

Belle Starr came to be known as the "female Jesse James." Though she was convicted for horse thievery (a serious charge in those days that could lead to execution), her reputation is mostly derived from the outlaw company she kept. Jesse James was one of the frequent visitors to the Starr home. It was a situation she once acknowledged in a letter, writing, "My home became known as an outlaw ranch."

Robert LeRoy Parker and Harry Alonzo Longabaugh, better known as Butch Cassidy and the Sundance Kid, led the notorious outlaw group called the Wild Bunch. They were so good at robbing trains that they also became known as the "Train Robbers' Syndicate." They eluded capture by Pinkerton detectives and other lawmen by staying in such colorfully named hideouts as Hole-in-the-Wall and Robber's Roost.

Another famous gang of outlaw brothers was the Daltons. Bob, Emmett, and Gratton Dalton achieved their crowning distinction in 1892, two years after the frontier was officially declared closed by the federal government. On October 5, 1892, the Dalton gang performed the most spectacular bank robbery in the West, simultaneously robbing two banks in Coffeyville, Kansas. The robbery failed when they were recognized and trapped in the banks by enraged townspeople, who grabbed rifles and pistols from nearby hardware stores and started shooting. After the gunfire stopped, a dozen men had been hit, Bob and Gratton were dead and dying, respectively, and three townspeople were fatally wounded. Emmett was shot and captured, sentenced to life in prison, and pardoned in 1907.

Emmett later had a career as a technical advisor for Hollywood westerns, and appeared in a few of the films as well. Recalling his days as an outlaw, he said that anyone who thought he could beat the law was "the biggest fool on earth."

Opposite: Robert Parker *(seated, far right)* and Harry Longabaugh *(seated, far left)*, photographed with members of the Wild Bunch, put together the longest run of successful bank and train robberies in the history of the American West.

THE WILD WEST IN POPULAR CULTURE

Above: Annie Oakley.

QUICK FACTS

⭐ Ned Buntline was called the "king of the dime novelists" because he was the most famous and most prolific of the genre writers. The customized Colt revolvers called Buntline Specials were named after him, though he had little to do with their design or distribution.

⭐ Buffalo Bill was given the Medal of Honor in 1872 for gallantry as an army scout. In 1917 it was revoked in a retroactive tightening of the qualification rules for the medal. In 1989 the rules were again rewritten, and the medal was restored to him.

⭐ Annie Oakley was not a Westerner. She was born in Ohio and spent most of her life in the East. After the United States entered World War I in 1917, Annie Oakley toured army camps, giving shooting instructions and demonstrations.

Americans who hungered for the freedom of wide-open spaces found it in the stories of the Wild West. The open prairie, where an individual could be his own boss, epitomized the American ideal to laborers living in crowded tenements in the East. Interest in the West, both real and romanticized, was fed by newspapers, books, and shows.

Hardly a week went by without a newspaper account of a new outbreak of hostile action by Indians, or a daring robbery by an outlaw. Real heroes, such as William "Buffalo Bill" Cody and James Butler "Wild Bill" Hickock, became living legends, thanks to inexpensive books, called "dime novels," that were printed by the millions. These books shamelessly blended fact and fiction to create lurid, action-packed adventures that, in the words of one dime-novel writer, offered "a thrill a page." Educators and religious leaders condemned the books as trash, but it did not stop their popularity.

Buffalo Bill was already famous when he started his Wild West show in 1882. He had been a Pony Express rider, a scout for the cavalry, and a buffalo hunter. To many he was the "best of the West." In 1882 he was asked to put on a special show for a Fourth of July celebration. The Old Glory Blow-Out featured target shooting, riding, bronco busting, a fast-paced roundup of cattle by horse-riding cowboys, and breathtaking trick shots of stunt marksmanship. The success of the show convinced Cody to turn it into what became Buffalo Bill's Wild West show.

In 1885, in one of his more dramatic efforts as a showman, Cody was able to persuade Chief Sitting Bull to participate. This was a risky move, because the Sioux chief had participated in the massacre of General George Armstrong Custer and his men at the Little Bighorn in 1876. When Cody introduced the chief for the first time, the audience booed. Fearing a riot, Cody quickly asked one of his star performers, trick shooter Annie Oakley, to begin her act. Annie was called a "shooting machine." Among her many stunts, she could hit a dime tossed in the air or slice a playing card in half with a bullet. Shortly after she began her act, Sitting Bull clapped and talked excitedly. An interpreter explained that Sitting Bull had never seen such extraordinary shooting. He was calling her "Watanya Cicilia"—Little Sure Shot. When the audience heard this, they cheered.

At the peak of the show's popularity, Cody had 640 performers and workers and hundreds of animals and vehicles. By the time Cody died in 1917, the show had lost its popularity.

Opposite: A poster advertising Buffalo Bill's Wild West show.

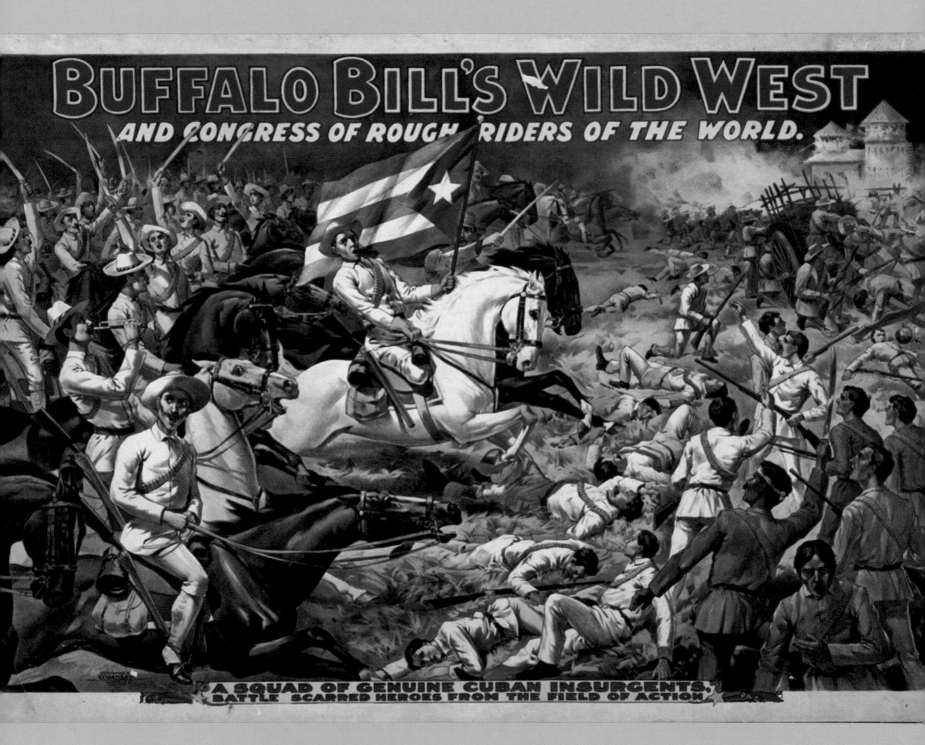

THE LAWMEN

Above: The logo of the Pinkerton Detective Agency stationery. Agents from the company were used to track down members of the James-Younger gang.

QUICK FACTS

⭐ In 1877 abolitionist Frederick Douglass became the first African American appointed to the post of U.S. marshal.

⭐ Judge Roy Bean was another of the many colorful lawmen of the West. According to one of the many tales about him, he once fined a corpse $40 for "carrying a concealed weapon."

⭐ Wyatt Earp said of Doc Holliday: "He was the most skillful gambler, and the nerviest, fastest, deadliest man with a six-gun I ever saw."

⭐ After touring with Buffalo Bill, Wild Bill Hickock returned to the West and lived in Deadwood, South Dakota. There he struck up a romance with another colorful character of the West, Calamity Jane. Hickock died as violently as he lived. He was shot from behind while playing poker. He was holding two pairs, aces and eights, which became known as the "dead man's hand."

Just as there were famous outlaws, there were also famous lawmen. They were the sheriffs, marshals, and deputies who apprehended, or more often than not, shot the outlaws they hunted. Among them were Wyatt Earp and his brothers Virgil and Morgan; John Henry "Doc" Holliday, who traded in his dentist's drill for a Colt six-shooter; Pat Garrett; Wild Bill Hickock; and Bass Reeves. Towns where they kept the peace were some of the most notorious in frontier history: Deadwood, South Dakota; Dodge City, Kansas; Tombstone, Arizona; and Cripple Creek, Colorado.

Deputy Marshal Bass Reeves was an African-American lawman who served on the Indian Territory in the 1870s and 1880s. According to homesteader Harve Lovelady, he was "the most feared U.S. marshal that was ever heard of in that country." Reeves was a big man and an excellent shot. Once while riding after outlaw Jim Webb, Reeves narrowly avoided getting himself killed. Webb's rifle shots hit Reeve's saddle horn, tore a button off his coat, and cut his bridle reins. The shoot-out ended when Reeves fired two bullets into Webb's chest, killing him.

The most famous of all gunfights between lawmen and outlaws took place on October 26, 1881 in Tombstone, Arizona. The gunfight at the O.K. Corral, as it came to be known, was between lawmen Wyatt, Virgil, and Morgan Earp and Doc Holliday, and outlaws Ike and Billy Clanton, Tom and Frank McLaury, and Billy Claiborne. The Clantons and McLaurys were ranchers who also weren't above rustling cattle and, according to rumor, other criminal activities. The Earps had been trying to stop their cattle-rustling operation, but had been unsuccessful in getting enough proof to jail them.

The gunfight began when City Marshal Virgil Earp and his deputies—that is, his brothers and Doc Holliday—confronted the Clantons, McLaurys, and Billy Claiborne at the corral. Wyatt said, "You've been looking for a fight and now you can have it." Virgil then ordered the group to raise their hands. Billy Clanton replied, "I don't want to fight." However, his actions seemed to contradict his words when, instead of raising his hands, he drew his pistol. Accounts claim the gunfire lasted less than a minute. When it was over, Tom and Frank McLaury were dead, Billy Clanton was dying, and Virgil, Morgan, and Doc Holliday were wounded. The gunfight at the O.K. Corral became such a legendary incident that it is reenacted to this day.

Opposite: The Dodge City Peace Commission pose in a photograph taken in the late 1870s. *(Seated, left to right)* Charlie Bassett, Wyatt Earp, M. F. McLane, and Neal Brown. *(Standing, left to right)* W. H. Harris, Luke Short, Bat Masterson, and W. F. Petillon.

THE INDIAN WARS IN THE NORTHERN PLAINS

Above: Lakota chiefs near Pine Ridge Indian Reservation.

QUICK FACTS

⭐ When different tribes encountered one another, they communicated using a system of gestures called Plains Sign Language (PSL). This language is based on approximately 80 gestures using one or both hands and contains a sophisticated grammatical structure.

⭐ Angela Haste Favell was 5 years old when she traveled by covered wagon to Wisconsin in 1856. She later wrote, "We had an Indian scare. For a while, we didn't know but we would all be scalped. There were a good many Indians roaming around, hunting and fishing, but they were always friendly. Now they acted differently They held powwows and war dances, and everybody thought that they were getting ready to massacre the white people. The Indian agent found that he couldn't control them . . . [a] messenger came and told us that the danger was over, that the Indians had promised they would not harm the whites."

Native American tribes conducted wars against one another differently from the way they waged war against white men. Often intertribal wars were campaigns designed to test the courage, intelligence, and skill of the young warriors who would later become tribal leaders. The act of war most admired by the tribe was not the killing of an enemy, but rather the striking of a blow on his body with a ceremonial stick, called a "coup stick," thus risking capture (and almost certain death). Also, wars were almost never conducted during winter, a time when all tribes focused their attention on fighting to survive the snow and bitter cold.

However, when the white man's cavalry and army waged war against the Indians, the intent was to capture or to kill. War was also waged during winter, and no distinction was made between peaceful tribes and hostile tribes. The unfortunate result was that out of desperation, otherwise peaceful tribes were sometimes driven into the camps of their hostile cousins out of a need for survival.

Occasionally different tribes would band together with a common cause: to fight the army and cavalry. However, because of the independent nature of the tribes, such alliances rarely lasted long. As the years passed, the Indians became more and more dependent on trade with the white men with whom they were fighting.

Chief Joseph (Hinmaton-Yalaktit or "Thunder Rolling From the Mountains") was a leader of the Nez Percé tribe, which lived in parts of Oregon, Idaho, and Wyoming. In an attempt to elude capture in 1877, he decided to lead his people to refuge in Canada. This fighting effort became an epic four-month, thirteen hundred-mile withdrawal. On September 30, in Montana just thirty miles from the Canadian border, Chief Joseph found himself surrounded. Unable to escape, he surrendered with the remnants of his tribe, saying, "It is cold and we have no blankets. . . . The little children are freezing to death. . . . Hear me . . . my heart is sick and sad. From where the sun now stands, I will fight no more against the white man." The tribe was taken to the Indian territory and Chief Joseph was sent to the Coleville Reservation, Washington, where he remained until his death in 1904.

Opposite: Chief Joseph of the Nez Percé.

SITTING BULL, CRAZY HORSE, AND THE SIOUX

Above: Sitting Bull.

QUICK FACTS

⭐ Native American boys did not receive a real name until they had a memorable dream or vision or did something noteworthy. Sitting Bull's name when he was young was "Slow," because he was so deliberate in his thoughts and actions.

⭐ During a raid against Fort Buford, Dakota Territory, Sitting Bull and his braves stole the large circular blade from the saw mill. They later used it as a drum.

⭐ Most nomadic Plains tribes were gathered into bands of a few hundred. Groups of more than 1,000 were rare. Gatherings of thousands of Indians occurred only for special ceremonies. The reason for this was that if the large groups stayed together too long, they would exhaust all the food in the area. A typical band used as many as 30,000 buffalo each year.

Sitting Bull and Crazy Horse are the most famous chiefs of the most famous of the Plains Indian nations—the Sioux. The Great Sioux nation in their language—Oceti Sakowin or "Seven Council Fires"— is a confederation of Native American bands and subbands that inhabited what is now North and South Dakota, and parts of Montana, Wyoming, Nebraska, and Minnesota. "Sioux" is condensed from "Nadousiouz," the name that was given by French explorers who encountered them in the 1600s. In their own language, which has three dialects, the Sioux call themselves "Dakota," "Nakota," and "Lakota."

The Sioux were more than just fierce nomadic horsemen. White men discovered that they knew how to defend their land both on the battlefield and in peaceful negotiations. The only reason the treaties signed by the Sioux later failed was because the white man lied.

The Oglala Sioux Crazy Horse (Tashunca-Uitco) was the greatest war chief of the Sioux nation. His successes against the U.S. cavalry in the Fetterman Fight at Fort Phil Kearny in 1866 (also known as the Fetterman Massacre), at the Hayfield Fight and the Wagon Box Fight in 1867, and at Little Bighorn in 1876, made him one of the most feared Indians in the West. However, his military victories only delayed his inevitable surrender. When the buffalo herds that were the Native Americans' livelihood vanished as a result of widespread slaughter by the white man, Crazy Horse was forced to take his starving people to a reservation. He surrendered to federal troops in 1877, but even on the reservation, he was regarded as a dangerous influence. On September 5, 1877, Crazy Horse was arrested. As he was being taken to jail, he tried to escape. He was fatally wounded during the attempt and soon died. He was thirty-six years old.

Sitting Bull (Tatanka Iyotake) was a Hunkpapa Sioux, who was both a war chief and a medicine man. Sitting Bull hated the white man just as much as Crazy Horse and fought just as hard to keep them out of Sioux land, especially the Black Hills of South Dakota, which were sacred to the Sioux. Nevertheless, like other hostile Indians, he was finally forced to take his followers to live on a reservation, which he did in 1883. Like Crazy Horse, he was regarded as a threat. On December 15, 1890, at the Standing Rock Indian Reservation in North Dakota, while he was being arrested, a gunfight broke out and he was shot to death.

Opposite: A group of Sioux warriors.

Above: A Civil War photograph of Custer.

QUICK FACTS

⭐ Custer's younger brother, Thomas, died at the Battle of the Little Bighorn. Tom had also had a distinguished military career during the Civil War. He was 1 of only 19 men to be awarded 2 Medals of Honor. When George was asked his opinion of his brother, he said: "If you want to know my opinion of Tom, I can only say that I think he should be the general and I the captain."

⭐ In 1874, Custer led an expedition to find a site for a military post into the Black Hills of what is now South Dakota. But the area was rumored to contain gold deposits, which Custer was also expected to confirm. When he returned, Custer said he had "found gold among the roots of the grass." Thousands of miners rushed into the region sacred to the Sioux. The resentment caused by Custer's expedition laid the foundation for what would become the Battle of Little Bighorn.

72

George Armstrong Custer was a dashing, famous Union cavalry hero when the Civil War ended. After the Civil War, he became a legendary Indian fighter. Because of his reputation, influential political figures in the East began to think of Custer as a candidate for president of the United States.

In the West, plans were being made for a campaign against the Native Americans in the late spring of 1876, which General Alfred Terry would lead into the southeastern Montana Territory, near the Little Bighorn River. The goal was to subdue three thousand hostile Indians camped there, composed of Sioux, led by Sitting Bull and Crazy Horse, and Cheyennes, led by Two Moons. By this time, Custer was a lieutenant colonel and commanding officer of the Seventh Cavalry. On June 22, he led more than five hundred men out of Fort Abraham Lincoln in what is now North Dakota, to the Little Bighorn.

As dawn broke on June 25, 1876, Mitch Bouyer and other scouts attached to Custer's command found the Native American camp. When they reported back to Custer, they advised him to wait for reinforcements. They had never seen so many Indians in one place before.

Custer rejected their advice and told everyone to get ready for battle. Custer divided his command into three parts, so that his forces could deliver a simultaneous three-prong attack. Major Marcus Reno would take 175 men and attack the camp from the south. Captain Frederick Benteen would attack from the west with 115 men. Custer would lead the largest prong, comprised of 225 men. They would assault a camp containing more than three thousand warriors.

When Crazy Horse heard the opening sounds of gunfire, he shouted, "Strong hearts, brave hearts, to the front! Weak hearts and cowards to the rear!" Leading the attack, Crazy Horse quickly drove back Reno's men, and in so doing he forced Benteen and his troops to rush to Reno's aid. Isolated and without any possibility of reinforcement, Custer and his men were massacred in less than an hour.

It was the most famous Indian military victory against the United States.

Opposite: A Wild West show re-creation of the death of Custer.

"Death of Custer"

THE BUFFALO SOLDIERS

Above: Pine Ridge Agency, South Dakota trooper, Buffalo Soldier Corporal.

QUICK FACTS

⭐ Originally the term "buffalo soldiers" applied only to the Ninth and Tenth Cavalry regiments. Later it came to include the infantry regiments as well.

⭐ Buffalo soldier Henry O. Flipper was the first African American to graduate from West Point in 1873.

⭐ First Sergeant Moses Williams was awarded the Medal of Honor, America's highest military award for valor, for his service in one of the campaigns against hostile Indians. His citation read, in part, that Williams "rallied a detachment, skillfully conducting a running fight of 3 or 4 hours, and by his coolness, bravery, and unflinching devotion to duty in standing by his commanding officer in an exposed position under a heavy fire from a large party of Indians saved the lives of at least 3 of his comrades."

The post–Civil War army had shrunk from a war-time high of 1.5 million men to only twenty-five thousand soldiers. Even though this small group no longer had to worry about a full-scale war, it still had a huge mission: to protect travelers, workers, and settlements in the entire western half of the United States, which included approximately 2.5 million miles of wilderness and sparsely populated land. On average, this left only one soldier for every one hundred square miles. In that uniformed group were four African-American regiments that comprised almost 15 percent of the total army.

"Buffalo soldiers," as they were called, got their nickname from the Native Americans. Accounts vary as to its exact origin, but all generally follow an account written by one officer's wife who said, "The Indians call them 'buffalo soldiers' because their wooly heads are so much like the matted cushion that is between the horns of the buffalo."

Just as they were during the Civil War, the units were racially segregated and commanded by white officers, reflecting the widespread and erroneous belief that African Americans did not have the mental capacity for leadership. The units were stationed across the frontier, and, like the white units, they laid telegraph lines, protected railroad construction crews, chased hostile Indians, and performed countless other tasks that helped make settlement of the frontier possible. In return they often encountered prejudice, hostility, discrimination, and violence from those they protected

Despite the bias, the buffalo soldiers did have their supporters. A Montana newspaper article reported, "The prejudice against colored soldiers seems to be without foundation. There are no better troops in the service." The buffalo soldiers carried out their duties with a commitment that earned the respect of their fellow white soldiers. Their desertion rate was lower than that of comparable white units, and reenlistment was above average. Part of the reason for this was that service in the army was seen as a path to progress and, ultimately, a better job. First Lieutenant John "Black Jack" Pershing, a white officer in the Tenth Cavalry, later wrote of his service with the unit, "I . . . knew that fairness and due consideration of their welfare would make the same appeal to them as to any other body of men. Most men, of whatever race, creed, or color, want to do the proper thing and they respect the man above him whose motive is the same."

Opposite: Buffalo soldiers of the 25th Infantry, some wearing buffalo robes, in Fort Keogh, Montana.

FRONTIER ARTS AND LETTERS

Above: Samuel Langhorn Clemens.

QUICK FACTS

☆ Samuel Clemens was a riverboat pilot on the Mississippi River before he went west. "Mark twain" is a riverboat expression used when checking the river's depth.

☆ Albert Bierstadt, who was born in Germany and immigrated to the United States, became famous for spectacular Western landscapes painted on gigantic canvases. One landscape, *The Rocky Mountains*, was painted on a 60-square-foot canvas. Bierstadt became so famous for his mountain landscapes that Mount Bierstadt in the Colorado Rockies was named for him.

☆ Another great painter of the West was Thomas Moran. The National Park Service considers him the father of the park system, because his painting *Grand Canyon of the Yellowstone* was instrumental in persuading Congress to create Yellowstone National Park, the nation's first national park.

The West attracted its share of writers, artists, and photographers who wanted to preserve a lifestyle and sights that they either sensed or knew would not last. Artist Charles M. Russell, who was also a cowboy, acknowledged this when he later recalled, "I'm glad I lived when I did—not twenty years later. I saw things when they were new." Another great Western artist, Frederick Remington, was even more blunt, stating, "I knew the wild riders and the vacant land were about to vanish forever—and the more I considered the subject, the bigger the forever loomed."

Most great writers of the West, including Willa Cather (*O! Pioneers*), Laura Ingalls Wilder (the Little House series), Owen Wister (*The Virginian*), and O. E. Rölvaag (*Giants in the Earth*) wrote about the West and the Great Plains well after the frontier had closed. The exception was Samuel Langhorn Clemens, better known as Mark Twain.

Clemens went west in 1861, accompanying his older brother, Orion, to Nevada, where Orion had accepted the position of secretary to the territorial governor. Samuel Clemens was twenty-seven years old and, like so many others who went West, hoped to make his fortune. He tried to become a lumber king only to see that plan literally go up in smoke when he accidentally set fire to his forest. Next came gold and silver prospecting and mining. Of those efforts, he later wrote, "We were stark mad with excitement—drunk with happiness—smothered under mountains of prospective wealth—arrogantly compassionate toward the plodding of millions who knew not our marvelous canyon—but our credit was not as good at the grocer's."

Clemens's string of failures ended when he accepted a job at the *Virginia City Territorial Enterprise*. Years later, Clemens recalled that when he began work for that newspaper, "I felt that I had found my legitimate occupation at last." Clemens wrote, often with embellishment, about local events and people. His first nationally famous work was *The Celebrated Jumping Frog of Calaveras County and Other Sketches*, which was published in 1867. Clemens would go on to achieve international fame as one of America's greatest writers with his novels *The Adventures of Tom Sawyer* and *The Adventures of Huckleberry Finn*. He recounted his misadventures in the West in his book *Roughing It* in which he made this observation, "Change is the handmaid Nature requires to do her miracles with."

Opposite: The Rocky Mountains by Albert Bierstadt, 1863.

Above: Three Navahos on horseback.

QUICK FACTS

⭐ Lieutenant General Philip Sheridan is credited with the statement, "The only good Indian is a dead Indian." It is actually a rewording of what he originally said when he was introduced to a group of Comanche that was surrendering. When Tosawi, a Comanche chief, was introduced to Sheridan, he said in broken English, "Tosawi, good Indian." Sheridan replied, "The only good Indians I ever saw were dead."

⭐ By the middle of the 1800s, the United States had 187 reservations containing 181,000 square miles of usually poor-quality land. Approximately 243,000 Indians were living on the reservations.

⭐ The Bureau of Indian Affairs was the government agency charged with administering the reservations. It controlled the supply and distribution of everything they needed from food, livestock, and crop seed to shelter, clothing, and fuel.

Though dry and rugged, the Southwest was home to a wide variety of Native American nations, including the Hopi, Mohave, Yuma, Zuni, Pueblo, Navaho, and Apache. Most of the tribes were peaceful, but two tribes—the Navaho and the Apache—violently resisted the encroachment of the white man onto the land.

The Navaho were a large tribe that lived along the Colorado River plateau region in and around northern Arizona. In the years before the Civil War, the relationship between the Navaho and the Americans was for the most part peaceful. However, that began to change when troops built Fort Defiance, the first in a series of forts on Navaho land. Fort Defiance was located on lush pastureland at the mouth of Canyon Bonito. In 1860 a herd of Navaho livestock wandered onto an unfenced meadow claimed by the soldiers. Instead of driving the herd away, a group of cavalry troopers killed the animals. The Navaho promptly raided the soldiers' herds to replace the lost horses and mules, thus beginning a yearlong season of harassment and reprisals that ultimately exhausted both sides. Peace followed for a number of months but did not last.

On September 22, 1861, a celebration at the recently erected Fort Wingate turned into a riot when the Navaho accused the soldiers of cheating in order to win the bets made on a horse race. Soldiers responded with their guns. Captain Nicholas Hodt, a witness to the incident, later wrote, "The Navaho, squaws, and children ran in all directions and were shot and bayoneted. . . ."

Brigadier General James Carleton arrived from California to assume command of the Department of New Mexico in 1862. Carlton was headstrong, ambitious, and ruthless, and he had a great hunger for land. When he saw the land of the Navaho, he called it "a princely realm, a magnificent pastoral and mineral country." He also regarded the Navaho as "wolves that run through the mountains," who had to be subdued. However, subjugation to him was the forcible removal of the Navaho from their ancestral land and relocation at the Bosque Redondo near the New Mexico-Texas border hundreds of miles away.

On June 23, 1863, he gave the commanding officer of Fort Wingate an ultimatum to deliver to the Navaho: "They can have until the twentieth of July of this year to come in—they and all those who belong to what they

Opposite: Navaho Indians at Fort Defiance.

Above: Ogala Sioux chiefs American Horse *(left)* and Red Cloud *(right)*, standing before a tepee.

call the peace party; *that after that day every Navaho that is seen will be considered as a hostile and treated accordingly*; that after that day the door now open will be closed." The deadline came and went, but no Navaho arrived at Fort Wingate. Carlton then ordered Colonel Kit Carson, who had gained fame in the region as a scout and Indian fighter, to take his men and round up the Navaho. When initial attempts to capture the Navaho failed, Carson issued orders to burn their crops and slaughter any Indian livestock they found in a "scorched earth" policy designed to deny the Navaho the opportunity to live off the land. In addition, Carlton issued a bounty of twenty dollars for every Navaho horse or mule and one dollar per head of sheep that soldiers brought to the fort. Inasmuch as soldiers earned less than twenty dollars per month, this was a powerful incentive for many. By early March 1864, almost all the Navaho had surrendered.

Shortly thereafter three different groups began what came to be called the "Long Walk of the Navaho" to their new home near Fort Sumner in the Bosque Redondo. The trek through the snow was grueling. An officer escorting one of the groups wrote, "On the second day's march, a very severe snowstorm set in which lasted for four days with unusual severity, and occasioned great suffering amongst the Indians, many of whom were nearly naked and of course unable to withstand such a storm." Hundreds of Navaho would die along the way.

Conditions in the Bosque Redondo were appalling. A. B. Norton, the agent assigned to oversee the Navaho, reported, "The water is black and brackish, scarcely bearable to the taste." He also noted that the soil was poor and unsuitable for farming and that the only wood available was mesquite, and that was twelve miles away from the village. He recommended, "The sooner [Bosque Redondo] is abandoned, the better." Norton's reports helped initiate an investigation, which led to the signing of a new treaty with the Navaho on June 1, 1868, that allowed them to return to their ancestral land. Of the journey back, Manuelito, one of the chiefs of the Navaho, said that as they neared their homeland, "we felt like talking to the ground, we loved it so, and some of the old men and women cried with joy when they reached their homes."

Opposite: A Navajo shaman gives medicine to another tribe member during a ceremony.

Above: Geronimo and some members of his tribe on their way to exile in Florida. Geronimo is in the front row, third from left *(circled)*. The young man to his left is his son.

QUICK FACTS

⭐ General Crook's reputation as an Indian fighter began in 1866 when he was made the commanding officer of the troops in Oregon. By 1870, he had subdued all the hostile tribes and demonstrated that he could ride, hunt, and shoot as well as any Indian. An aide during this period wrote in admiration, "He knew the Indian better than the Indian did."

⭐ A number of Indian reform groups in the East began as a result of negative reports about treatment of the Native Americans. One of the groups was led by Vincent Colyer, whom Arizona newspaper editors had scornfully nicknamed "Vincent the Good." The reform groups' "do-good" efforts were regarded with cynicism by many who lived near the reservations, as almost all tribes east of the Mississippi River had been exterminated.

General George Crook, the army's most skilled Indian fighter, called the Apaches "the tigers of the human species." By the late 1800s there were only about eight thousand Apaches divided into such tribes as the Jicarilla, Mescalero, White Mountain, and Chiricahua. The Apaches were as tough and untamable as their homeland and were regarded as the greatest guerrilla fighters in the world.

The Apache had a number of important chiefs who fought the armies of Mexico and the United States, including Cochise, Nana, and Victorio. The last and most famous of them was Geronimo, a man known to his people as Goyathlay. In 1858, Mexican soldiers killed his mother, wife, and children. From then on, he fought a campaign of retribution that made him the most dangerous man in the Southwest.

In 1886 the army embarked on a campaign to capture or kill Geronimo. Five thousand cavalry, five hundred scouts from other Apache tribes, and thousands more militia troops began a summerlong campaign to find him. For weeks Geronimo and the small group of braves with him roamed the ancestral Apache lands, eluding not only the American troops, but also thousands of Mexican soldiers who hunted him whenever he crossed the border into Mexico. Finally he and his men were found by the Apache scouts Martine and Kayitah, and cavalry Lieutenant Charles Gatewood, whom the Apaches called "Big Nose Captain." Geronimo knew Gatewood and respected him. Geronimo said, "I give myself up to you. . . . Once I moved about like the wind. Now I surrender to you and that is all." But Geronimo's surrender opened a new chapter of tragedy in the life of his followers. He, the men with him, and their families were taken into military custody and shipped to Marion, Florida.

Many died as a result of diseases native to the humid, tropical climate, which was so different from their desert homeland. Their children were taken from them and boarded in an Indian school that had been established at Carlisle, Pennsylvania. There, many Apache children died of sickness. Eventually the Kiowa and Comanche, traditional enemies of the Apache, learned of the plight of Geronimo and his people and offered them a portion of their reservation to live on. In 1894 Geronimo and his group were permitted to go there. Geronimo died in 1909, still a prisoner of war of the U.S. government.

Opposite: Geronimo *(center)* and members of his band.

Above: Bodies of Sioux men, women, and children killed at Wounded Knee.

QUICK FACTS

⭐ Dances were an important part of Native American life and religion. There were dances to celebrate successful buffalo hunts, the changing of the seasons, and peaceful meetings between tribes during councils.

⭐ One of the most famous dances was the Sun Dance. Its purpose was to inspire dreams or visions. Sun Dance participants would take part in a ritual that usually lasted four days. During that time, they would not eat or drink. They performed ritual motions, blowing through an eagle-bone whistle while they stared at a symbolic object, like a buffalo skull placed on top of a tall pole. Some Sun Dance participants submitted to ritual torture in order to inspire a dream or vision.

One of the most tragic chapters in the history of the Native Americans in the United States was the Ghost Dance movement that took place as the frontier was closing. This religious movement was based on the belief that if the Indians performed Ghost Dance songs and dances, the white man would disappear, dead Indians would be resurrected, the buffalo herds would return, and the old Indian way of life would be restored.

The Ghost Dance began in 1870 in Nevada. Tavibo, a prophet in the Northern Paiute tribe, founded the movement that soon spread through Nevada, California, and Oregon. When his prophecies failed to occur, the movement seemed to die, but then in 1889, another Paiute, Wovoka, revived it. In his speeches he said, "All Indians must dance, everywhere, keep on dancing. . . . When Great Spirit comes this way, then all the Indians go to mountains, high up away from whites. . . . Then while Indians way up high, big flood comes like water and all white people die, get drowned. After that, water go away and then nobody but Indians everywhere and game all kinds thick."

Two Sioux—Kicking Bear and Short Bull—heard of Wovoka's preachings and visited him to learn more. When they returned, they told Sitting Bull and other Sioux what they had heard and seen. In addition Kicking Bear said that if they wore sacred garments painted with magic symbols— Ghost Shirts—bullets from white man's guns would not harm them. Though it was a peaceful movement that called for its followers not to "do harm to anyone," the movement struck fear in the federal reservation agents and other whites responsible for Indian affairs, as well as in those living near Sioux reservations. Government agent James McLaughlin, known to the Sioux as White Hair, was one of many whites who believed that if the Indians were to survive, they must reject their old ways of living and be assimilated into the civilization of the white man. The Ghost Dance was a threat to this movement, because it advocated a return to the old ways. Also, the whites believed that the Ghost Dance movement would lead to another Indian uprising. One panic-stricken agent telegraphed to his superiors, "We need protection and we need it now. The [Ghost Dance leaders] should be arrested and confined at some military post until the matter is quieted, and this should be done at once." At the time, Sitting

Opposite: Indians performing a Ghost Dance before Wounded Knee.

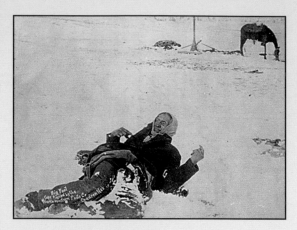

Above: Big Foot, leader of the Sioux, lies frozen in the battlefield where he died.

Bull was living on the Standing Rock Reservation in North Dakota. In order to prevent him from adding his support to the movement, General Nelson Miles ordered Sitting Bull's arrest on December 12, 1890. Three days later, forty-three Indian police officers, backed by a squadron of U.S. cavalry, arrived at Sitting Bull's cabin. A large crowd of Ghost Dancers arrived before the Indian police could leave with Sitting Bull. An argument broke out. Shots were fired. Within minutes Sitting Bull was dead.

More violence was to come. Hundreds of Sioux on the Standing Rock Reservation fled, seeking refuge in various Ghost Dance camps, or at the Pine Ridge Reservation in South Dakota where the last great chief of the Sioux, Red Cloud, lived. Sioux chief Big Foot led a group of 350 people to Pine Ridge, but Big Foot had been listed by the government as one of the "fomenters of disturbances." His band, composed mostly of women and children, was intercepted three days after Christmas by Major Samuel Whitside and his men of the Seventh Cavalry. Whitside had orders to escort Big Foot and his band to a camp at Wounded Knee Creek where their horses and guns would be confiscated. Once the group had arrived at Wounded Knee, the troopers began searching for weapons. In the midst of all this, some of the Sioux began a Ghost Dance. During the search, which yielded few weapons, a fight broke out between one of the Sioux warriors and several cavalry troopers. Once again, shooting started, this time with machine guns. Louise Weasel Bear, a survivor, later recalled, "We tried to run, but they shot us like we were a buffalo."

When it was over, 153 Indians lay dead. A number of the wounded crawled away and died later. Of the 350 Sioux, an estimated 300 were killed. Among the cavalry, twenty-five died and thirty-nine were wounded, most of them hit by friendly fire. The Ghost Dance movement soon ended. A result of the tragedy was voiced by Black Elk, a Sioux holy man, who said of the massacre at Wounded Knee, "Something else died there in the bloody mud, and was buried in the blizzard. A people's dream died there."

Opposite: U.S. troops inspect a vanquished tribe, days after battle at Wounded Knee.

Above: A Currier and Ives lithograph titled *Course of Empire* that shows the railroad and the advance of the white man into the frontier.

QUICK FACTS

⭐ On July 12, 1893, University of Wisconsin history professor Frederick Jackson Turner in a meeting of the American Historical Association remarked, "To the frontier the American intellect owes its striking characteristics . . . coarseness and strength combined with acuteness and inquisitiveness; that practical, inventive turn of mind . . . that restless, nervous energy; that dominant individualism . . . and withal that buoyancy and exuberance that comes with freedom."

⭐ The records of the 1890 census were almost totally destroyed in a fire on January 10, 1921. Only 6,160 names from 10 states and the District of Columbia, along with a separate list of military veterans and their widows that was kept in a different building, survived.

When the early leaders of the United States wrote the Constitution, they included a section that called for a census, or counting, of the population to be taken every ten years. The purpose of it was to revise and update congressional voting districts to make sure there was fair representation of the people in the House of Representatives and in the electoral college, which elects the president. The U.S. Census Bureau conducted its first census in 1790, recording that the nation had 3.9 million people. In that first census the bureau also calculated population density. Areas that had an average population of two people per square mile or fewer were identified as "wilderness." The first "frontier line," as it came to be called, started in the middle of the coast of Maine, went inland a few miles, then went southwest through the middle of New York and Virginia, ending in Georgia.

According to the second census, which had been taken in 1800, the population was a little more than 5.3 million and the frontier line had moved west, but not by much. When President Thomas Jefferson bought the Louisiana Purchase from France in 1803, he estimated that it would take a hundred generations for the new frontier to be filled.

However, Jefferson had no way of knowing of the population boom that would occur. Though a man of great imagination, he could not dream of the waves of immigrants that would come from across the oceans. These people included Carl Schurz from Germany, who would become a famous newspaper publisher, and eighteen-year-old Léon Charles Fouquet from France who, when he saw his ship arrive in New York City harbor wrote, "Land! Land! Hurrah! Hurrah for America, my free country! I was jubilant. Everyone on board was jubilant." Fouquet went on to settle in Kansas.

These, and so many others, ventured to every corner of the country, starting new lives. The eleventh census was taken in 1890. After the results had been tabulated, the superintendent of the Census Bureau issued a statement: The frontier was closed. It had taken fewer than three generations for the population to increase enough to establish settlements in every part of the country. An epic chapter in American history had ended, but its influence had not.

Opposite: A photograph taken the instant the signal was given to begin the rush to claim land in Oklahoma, the former Indian Territory.

GLOSSARY

Abolition—The act of eliminating slavery.

Abolitionist—Someone who believes in eliminating slavery.

Acquittal—A decision given by a judge or jury that declares that an individual is not guilty of the crimes charged.

Alliance—An association of two or more individuals, groups, or nations who agree to cooperate to achieve a common goal.

Amnesty—A general pardon from crimes issued by the president of the United States or a state governor.

Assassination—The murder of a public official or an important individual.

Band—A group of people who have the same ideas or beliefs, or who are pursuing the same activity together.

Bright's disease—A dangerous inflammation of the kidney.

Campaign—A series of military operations undertaken to achieve a specific goal in a war.

Carpetbagger—A Northerner holding a government position in the South during the period of Reconstruction. It refers to the fact that some men were in such a rush to go to the South and exploit the situation for their own gain that they hurriedly packed all their belongings into one piece of luggage known as a "carpetbag."

Cavalry—Combat troops mounted on horses.

Census—The official counting of the people by the government in order to collect statistics about the population and to help determine voting representation.

Commission—A fee paid to an agent or employee for transacting a piece of business or performing a service; especially a percentage of the money received paid to the agent responsible for the business.

Confederacy—Officially the Confederate States of America, the group of Southern states that seceded from the United States of America in 1860 and 1861. This included Alabama, Arkansas, Florida, Georgia, Louisiana, Mississippi, North Carolina, South Carolina, Tennessee, Texas, and Virginia.

Confederate—In the Civil War, any Southerner who sided with the Confederacy, especially a soldier or sailor of the military.

Confiscate—The government seizure of private property, usually as a penalty.

Constitution—In the United States, it is a document composed of seven articles with amendments that forms the supreme law of the Federal government.

Contraband—During the Civil War, a slave who successfully reached Union lines or territory held by the Union army.

Depression—In economics, a period in which a region or nation suffers a significant increase in unemployment and poverty.

Election—The selection by the majority of a popular vote for individuals wishing to hold public office.

Emancipation Proclamation—President Abraham Lincoln's official declaration that freed the slaves.

Enfranchisement—To free from slavery or to admit to citizenship and give the right to vote.

Expedition—A journey made by an organized group for a specific purpose, usually exploration or scientific study.

Fortification—Defenses, usually walls and trenches, constructed to add strength and protection to a military position.

Freedman—During Reconstruction, an individual legally released from slavery or bondage.

Fugitive Slave Law—The act of Congress in 1850 that ordered the return of runaway slaves from any state to which they had fled.

Guerrilla—A member of a group of irregular soldiers, usually volunteers, who make surprise hit-and-run raids against regular army supply lines or encampments.

Homestead—A tract of public land granted by the United States government to a settler to be developed as a farm.

Homestead Act—An act of Congress passed in 1862 granting public land, usually in the amount of one hundred and sixty acres, to any citizen or alien intending to become a citizen, to be developed as a farm.

Impeachment—The formal removal of a political figure from public office.

Inauguration—A ceremony that formally, and usually publicly, gives to an individual the authority to hold a particular public office.

Infantry—Soldiers trained to fight and travel on foot.

Moderate—Someone who holds views, usually political views, that are not strongly for or against a particular issue.

Nationalism—A devotion to one's nation; patriotism.

Nomad—A group or individual who move from place to place seasonally.

Powwow—Among North American Indians, a ceremonial meeting among a group of Native American tribes or nations at select sites.

Reconstruction—The process of reorganizing and re-admitting the Southern states that had seceded from the Union.

Refugee—Somebody who is seeking safety and protection from war, persecution, or natural disaster.

Reservation—An area of land set aside by the United States government for a particular purpose, usually for use by the Native Americans, especially in North America.

Scalawag—During Reconstruction, a Southerner who was a Republican and who usually held a government position in the South.

Secede—To break away or leave an organization. In the Civil War the act of states from the South choosing to leave the United States to form the Confederate States of America.

Segregation—The separation of a race or group from the rest of society.

Shaman—A Native American holy man who is respected for his powers of healing and prophecy.

Sodbuster—A slang expression for a farmer, particularly on the Great Plains.

Suffrage—The right to vote.

Telegraph—A method of long-distance communication using coded electric impulses transmitted through wires.

Tenement—A piece of property used by one person, but owned by another, usually referring to an apartment building.

Territory—A region of the United States that is not part of any state and is governed by a legislature that is organized by, but independent from, the federal government.

Treaty—A formal written agreement between two or more nations.

Typhoid fever—A highly infectious, often fatal, disease transmitted by contaminated food or water.

Union—During the Civil War, the states in the North that did not secede to form the Confederacy.

BIBLIOGRAPHY

Ambrose, Stephen E. *Crazy Horse and Custer: The Parallel Lives of Two American Warriors*. New York: Anchor Books, 1996.

_____. *Nothing Like It in the World: The Men Who Built the Transcontinental Railroad, 1863–1869*. New York: Simon & Schuster, 2000.

Beschloss, Michael, ed. *The American Heritage Illustrated History of the Presidents*. New York: Crown Publishers, 2000.

Block, Eugene B. *Great Train Robberies of the West*. New York: Coward-McCann, 1959.

Brown, Dee. *Bury My Heart at Wounded Knee: An Indian History of the American West*. New York: Henry Holt, 2001.

Clark, Thomas D., and Albert D. Kirwan. *The South Since Appomattox: A Century of Regional Change*. New York: Oxford University Press, 1967.

Conlan, Roberta, ed. *The Wild West*. New York: Time-Life Books, 1993.

Forbis, William H. *The Old West: The Cowboys*. New York: Time-Life Books, 1973.

Hakim, Joy. *Reconstructing America*. New York: Oxford University Press, 2003.

Heidler, David S., and Jeanne T. Heidler, eds. *Encyclopedia of the American Civil War: A Political, Social, and Military History*. New York: W. W. Norton & Co., 2000.

Johnson, Thomas H., ed. *The Oxford Companion to American History*. New York: Oxford University Press, 1966.

Kinsley, D. A. *Custer: Favor the Bold: Custer: The Civil War Years*. New York: Holt, Reinhart and Winston, 1967.

Kraft, Louis. *Gatewood & Geronimo*. Albuquerque: University of New Mexico Press, 2000.

McPherson, James M. *Battle Cry of Freedom: The Civil War Era*. New York: Oxford University Press, 1988.

_____. *Ordeal by Fire: The Civil War and Reconstruction*. New York: McGraw-Hill, 1992.

Nevin, David. *The Old West: The Expressmen*. New York: Time-Life Books, 1974.

_____. *The Old West: The Soldiers*. New York: Time-Life Books, 1973.

O'Connor, Richard. *Black Jack Pershing*. Garden City, New York: Doubleday, 1961.

O'Neal, Bill, James A. Crutchfield, and Dale L. Walker. *The Wild West*. Lincolnwood, Illinois: Publications International, 2001.

Reiter, Joan Swallow. *The Old West: The Women*. New York: Time-Life Books, 1978.

Ward, Geoffrey C. *The West: An Illustrated History*. Boston: Little, Brown, 1996.

Wishart, David J., ed. *Encyclopedia of the Great Plains*. Lincoln: University of Nebraska Press, 2004.

AMERICAN FRONTIER WEB SITES

Reconstruction and the frontier of the American West were extraordinary, wrenching, and dynamic periods in our history. The Internet offers many opportunities to discover more about a time that continues to influence us. One of the best places to go are state and local historical societies, which are dedicated in recording, preserving, and recounting through Web sites, museums, and exhibitions on their state and local heritage. Here are a few of the many sites available:

Library of Congress
www.loc.gov

Montana Historical Society
www.his.state.mt.us

U.S. Census Bureau
www.census.gov

Nebraska Historical Society
www.nebraskahistory.org

National Park Service
www.nps.gov

Historical Society of New Mexico
www.hsnm.org

Bureau of Indian Affairs
www.doi.gov/bureau-indian-affairs.html

Nevada Department of Cultural Affairs
www.dmla.clan.lib.nv.us

Buffalo Bill Historical Center
www.bbhc.org

Historical Society of North Dakota
www.state.nd.us/hist

Museum of the American West
www.autry-nationalcenter.org/index_gp.php

Oklahoma Historical Society
www.ok-history.mus.ok.us

Arizona Historical Society
www.arizonahistoricalsociety.org

Oregon Historical Society
www.ohs.org

California Historical Society
www.californiahistoricalsociety.org

Texas State Historical Association
www.tsha.utexas.edu/links

Colorado Historical Society
www.coloradohistory.org

Utah State Historical Society
www.history.utah.gov

Idaho State Historical Society
www.idahohistory.net

Washington State Historical Society
www.wshs.org

Kansas State Historical Society
www.kshs.org

Wyomin State Historical Society
www.wyshs.org

INDEX

94

95

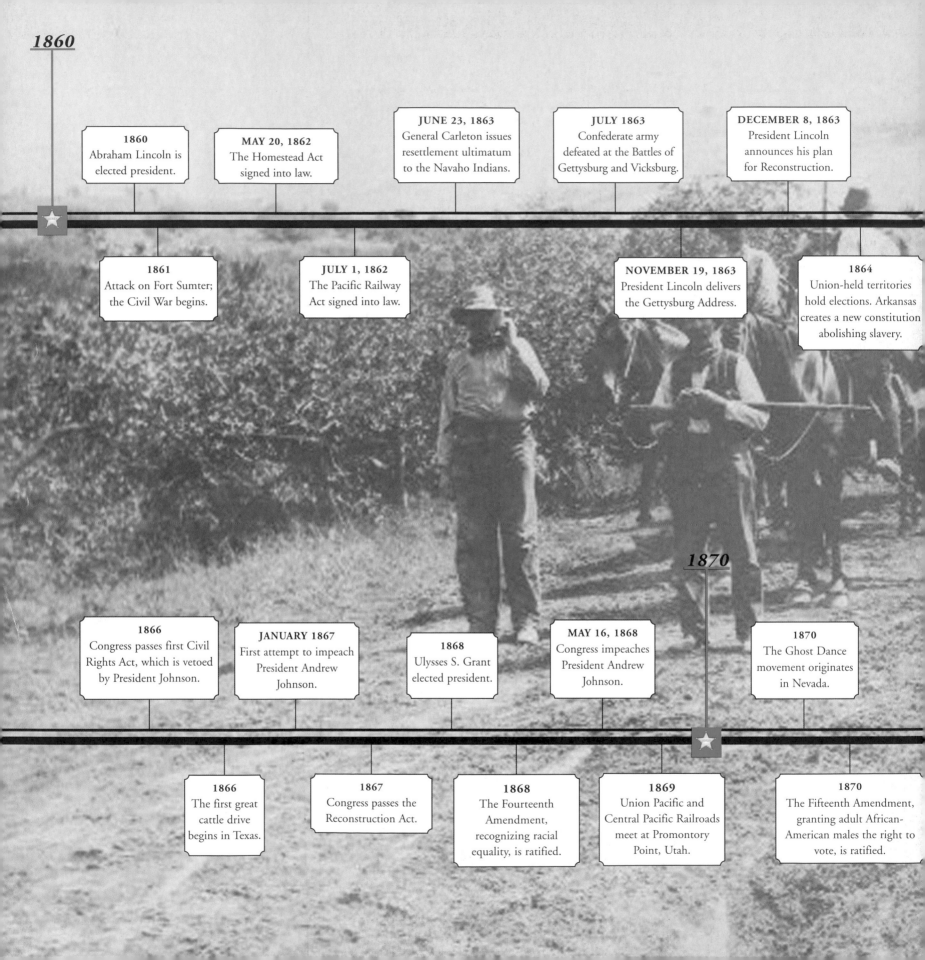

1860

1860
Abraham Lincoln is elected president.

MAY 20, 1862
The Homestead Act signed into law.

JUNE 23, 1863
General Carleton issues resettlement ultimatum to the Navaho Indians.

JULY 1863
Confederate army defeated at the Battles of Gettysburg and Vicksburg.

DECEMBER 8, 1863
President Lincoln announces his plan for Reconstruction.

1861
Attack on Fort Sumter; the Civil War begins.

JULY 1, 1862
The Pacific Railway Act signed into law.

NOVEMBER 19, 1863
President Lincoln delivers the Gettysburg Address.

1864
Union-held territories hold elections. Arkansas creates a new constitution abolishing slavery.

1870

1866
Congress passes first Civil Rights Act, which is vetoed by President Johnson.

JANUARY 1867
First attempt to impeach President Andrew Johnson.

1868
Ulysses S. Grant elected president.

MAY 16, 1868
Congress impeaches President Andrew Johnson.

1870
The Ghost Dance movement originates in Nevada.

1866
The first great cattle drive begins in Texas.

1867
Congress passes the Reconstruction Act.

1868
The Fourteenth Amendment, recognizing racial equality, is ratified.

1869
Union Pacific and Central Pacific Railroads meet at Promontory Point, Utah.

1870
The Fifteenth Amendment, granting adult African-American males the right to vote, is ratified.